"With scriptural insights and practical ⸺, ⸺ Haase reminds us that God has an ardent longing for a deeper and deeper relationship with each of us. The disciple's journey is a mystical journey that leads to a deeper experience of the ordinary and mundane. To plumb the depths of the secular is to scale the heights of the sacred. An authentic expression of the Franciscan vision of the world!"

Richard Rohr, Center for Action and Contemplation

"In *Becoming an Ordinary Mystic*, Father Haase has painted a sublimely practical picture of what it might look like to pursue life with Christ in the details of commonplace living. This book is an encouragement to live in the now, reflect on the why, and live purposefully in his presence."

Manuel Luz, creative arts pastor, author of *Honest Worship*

"A deeply personal and intimate look at what it means to be a mystic. Father Albert invites us to dive deep and unlock the mysteries of our faith. If we are willing to make the descent, Father Albert guides all of us on an adventure rooted in the depths of our heart. It is simple, insightful, and life giving."

Chuck Neff, host of The Inner Life, Relevant Radio

"Franciscan Albert Haase is a master storyteller. Throughout *Becoming an Ordinary Mystic* his pithy, down-to-earth anecdotes draw a reader in. But these tales have a decided plumb line. Into them he skillfully weaves insights from Christian wisdom figures—from Job to Teresa of Ávila to Thomas Merton. What emerges is a surprisingly accessible guide to a mature Christian life saturated with the divine presence. The author gives thoughtful attention to classic spiritual arts of awareness, listening, attentiveness, forgiveness, apophatic and kataphatic prayer as well as experiences of dark night, sin, fear, doubt, and mercy, all while grounding enduring truths in real life using arresting allusions to Haase's own struggles and the struggles of those he ministered to."

Wendy M. Wright, professor emerita of theology, Creighton University

"Albert Haase holds keen insight for the subtleties of the spiritual journey. His guidance gently leads us along the path that makes meaning out of our life."

Phileena Heuertz, founding partner of Gravity, a Center for Contemplative Activism, author of *Mindful Silence* and *Pilgrimage of a Soul*

"Belief does not come as naturally for many of us as it did for our parents and grandparents. A world without God seems a live option. So if we are to believe, we will need to be people who have experienced a living God, people who are ordinary mystics. With lucidity, candor, and warmth, Father Haase helps us understand that while being an ordinary mystic isn't necessarily easy, it is simple, and he shows us how to become one."

Austin Fischer, lead pastor of Vista Community Church, author of *Faith in the Shadows*

"Want to be a mystic? I didn't, until I read what Father Albert has to say about this surprisingly accessible way of perceiving the road we're traveling. In this short book, you'll find yourself reading along with some of the greatest minds of the church. You'll recognize yourself in the stories, grow through the training exercises, and be inspired by the invitation to claim your inner mystic. And will you become, in the end, one of those blessed ones? That's up to you."

Alice Camille, coauthor of *Fearless: Stories of the American Saints*

"We are mystics because we are called to a relationship with God and to live that intimacy God desires with every person. So this is the book many folks have been waiting for. In ordinary language with great examples and stories of real people, Father Haase leads us to understand the spiritual journey in ways that truly touch the heart. Each chapter concludes with an exercise to practice, reflect, and ponder, which I found very helpful. Surely most of us want to become ordinary mystics and this work encourages us to continue seeking the deeper life with God."

Joseph Tedesco, superior of Mepkin Abbey Trappist Monastery, Moncks Corner, SC

Becoming
an
ORDINARY
Mystic

SPIRITUALITY FOR THE REST OF US

ALBERT HAASE, OFM

An imprint of InterVarsity Press
Downers Grove, Illinois

InterVarsity Press
P.O. Box 1400, Downers Grove, IL 60515-1426
ivpress.com
email@ivpress.com

*InterVarsity Press® is the book-publishing division of InterVarsity Christian Fellowship/USA®, a movement of
students and faculty active on campus at hundreds of universities, colleges, and schools of nursing in the United States
of America, and a member movement of the International Fellowship of Evangelical Students. For information about
local and regional activities, visit intervarsity.org.*

Cover design and image composite: Cindy Kiple
Interior design: Daniel van Loon
Images: © Dirk Wustenhagen / Trevillion Images

ISBN 978-0-8308-4657-3 (print)
ISBN 978-0-8308-7057-8 (digital)

Library of Congress Cataloging-in-Publication Data

A catalog record for this book is available from the Library of Congress.

P 25 24 23 22 21 20 19 18 17 16 15 14 13 12 11 10 9 8 7 6 5 4 3 2 1

Y 38 37 36 35 34 33 32 31 30 29 28 27 26 25 24 23 22 21 20 19

The devout Christian of the future will either be a "mystic," one who has experienced "something," or he will cease to be anything at all.

KARL RAHNER

OTHER BOOKS AND MEDIA BY ALBERT HAASE, OFM

Swimming in the Sun: Rediscovering the Lord's Prayer with
Francis of Assisi and Thomas Merton
St. Anthony Messenger Press, 1993

Enkindled: Holy Spirit, Holy Gifts, coauthored with Bridget Haase, OSU
St. Anthony Messenger Press, 2001

Instruments of Christ: Reflections on the Peace
Prayer of St. Francis of Assisi
St. Anthony Messenger Press, 2004

Coming Home to Your True Self: Leaving the Emptiness of False Attractions
InterVarsity Press, 2008

Living the Lord's Prayer: The Way of the Disciple
InterVarsity Press, 2009

The Lord's Prayer: A Summary of the Entire Gospel
(Five CDs) NowYouKnowMedia.com, 2010

This Sacred Moment: Becoming Holy Right Where You Are
InterVarsity Press, 2011

The Life of Antony of Egypt: by Athanasius, A Paraphrase
InterVarsity Press, 2012

Catching Fire, Becoming Flame: A Guide for Spiritual Transformation
Paraclete Press, 2013

Catching Fire, Becoming Flame: A Guide for Spiritual Transformation
(DVD) Paraclete Press, 2013

Keeping the Fire Alive: Navigating Challenges in the Spiritual Life
(DVD) Paraclete Press, 2014

Come, Follow Me: Six Responses to the Call of Jesus
(DVD) Paraclete Press, 2014

Saying Yes: Discovering and Responding to God's Will in Your Life
Paraclete Press, 2016

Saying Yes: What is God's Will for Me?
(DVD) Paraclete Press, 2016

The BE Attitudes: Ten Paths to Holiness
(DVD) Paraclete Press, 2019

Practical Holiness: Pope Francis as Spiritual Companion
Paraclete Press, 2019

CONTENTS

INTRODUCTION

I was ten years old. I was sitting on the floor of my bedroom and paging through a picture book about the lives of the saints. It was December 14. I know the date because I distinctly remember turning to that day's page to see whose feast day the Catholic Church celebrated. I remember scratching my head over the first sentence about that day's saint: "Saint John of the Cross was a Carmelite mystic of the sixteenth century." I was old enough to know the Carmelites were a religious order like the Franciscans, Dominicans, and Benedictines. But a mystic?

Later that day, I asked my mother, "What's a mystic?"

My mother was accustomed to answering my precocious questions. "That's a special friend of God."

"I want to be one!" I instantly blurted out, knowing that being a *special* friend of God would be like what I had with my best friend, Dennis, who lived across the street.

"It doesn't quite happen like that," she said. "You don't choose to be one. You are chosen."

I didn't believe her. I was determined to become a special friend of God and would spend the subsequent years trying to prove her wrong.

Twenty years later, I sat with my spiritual director. It was one of those days—I was a bit discouraged. After telling him about that first childhood encounter with John of the Cross and my reaction to my mother's comment, I began to think out loud:

- I should be further along on the spiritual journey.
- Why don't I see any progress?
- What am I doing wrong?

After twenty years of trying to be chosen as a special friend of God, I felt like I was just walking in spiritual circles.

"Now I understand why St. Teresa of Avila, having been knocked out of her carriage and fallen into a water puddle, said, 'O God, if this is how you treat your friends, no wonder they are so few!'"

"But, Albert," my spiritual director replied, "Teresa of Avila was a mystic. That's how mystics sometimes feel. And I suspect, because you're feeling the way you do, you're a mystic too. We're all called to be mystics."

Me, a mystic? Had I been chosen as a special friend of God and not known it?

He continued, "In every moment of our lives, God is asking us to respond to grace—and grace is simply God's ardent longing and enthusiastic invitation to a deeper relationship, a mystical relationship. Mystics are ordinary Christians who do what we are all called to do, respond to grace. I know you well enough to know you are intentional about prayer. So you're responding to God's invitation to spend time with him. You're deliberate about doing acts of charity. So you are responding to God's call to move beyond your selfishness. You make an annual retreat. You keep working at forgiveness. And you keep trying to become more attentive and sensitive to what God is asking of you. I think it's safe to say you've been chosen like everyone else to be a 'special friend of God,' as your mother called it. You're an ordinary mystic."

A-n o-r-d-i-n-a-r-y m-y-s-t-i-c. I had to let the words sink in. I never would have known it but it certainly now made sense.

Even while naively trying to make myself worthy of being chosen, I had mistakenly thought mysticism meant acquiring esoteric knowledge or having rarefied experiences—but where were the wisdom and the supersized feelings? That's why I was discouraged.

After more than thirty years since sitting down with that spiritual director, I've discovered mysticism is more commonplace than I originally thought. It is living with sensitivity to the divine presence and responding to God's ardent longing and enthusiastic invitation to a deeper relationship at this very moment: in a burning bush as happened to Moses, in the tiny whisper of a sound as Elijah experienced, in the call to come out of hiding like Zacchaeus, in the mysterious stranger who suddenly appears and offers hope as one did with two disciples walking to Emmaus.

Mystics teach us to celebrate Jesus' offer of forgiveness right here, right now, and not live in the past, submerged in guilt over sinful actions. Mystics have distractions in prayer—Teresa of Avila mentions times when, during prayer, her attention was focused more on the grains of sand in the hourglass than the crucifix—but they acknowledge and respect distractions as potential teachers in the spiritual life. Mystics pray from their current feelings, even the ones other people consider inappropriate to express to God—think again of Teresa falling out of the carriage. Mystics sometimes lose the feeling of having God in their life—John of the Cross called it the "dark night," and Mother Teresa of Calcutta experienced it for almost fifty years. Mystics are waitresses, welders, writers, and web designers who heartily respond to the direct and enthusiastic invitation of

Jesus, "Come, follow me." It's the ordinary call singularly offered to all. The mystics' journey is, in fact, the disciples' journey: "We're all called to be mystics," as my spiritual director said.

There are many ordinary mystics in these pages who have taught me about spiritual formation and the mystical journey. Some are friends. Some are spiritual directees. A few have been my spiritual directors. I've changed their names and details to ensure their privacy. I've done my best to pass along their wisdom and teachings.

At the end of each chapter you'll find a set of exercises—Practice, Reflect, and Ponder. I encourage you to take a bit of time with each of them. You might want to use the Practice technique to enrich your toolbox of spiritual formation. You can journal through the Reflect questions and share your answers with your spiritual director. A book study or spiritual formation group will come up with other ways to experience the teachings found in each chapter. A helpful way to conclude each group session would be to sit in silence for five minutes with the summary sentence found in the Ponder section.

If you want a deeper appreciation for God's ardent longing and enthusiastic invitation to a deeper relationship, this is the book for you. You might be surprised to discover that, without even knowing it, you've been chosen as a special friend of God. Perhaps you don't have highfalutin thoughts or ecstatic experiences—most of us don't. You just try every day to listen to God's invitation and respond to it. And that's the secret: like Moses, Elijah, Zacchaeus, and the disciples on the road to Emmaus, God is again inviting you to notice the extraordinary in the ordinary, the sacred in the secular, and the mystical in the mundane—to become an ordinary mystic.

Chapter 1

RIGHT HERE, RIGHT NOW

MINDFULNESS BREEDS MYSTICISM

I had just flown back to Texas the night before, and here I was again at the Dallas–Ft. Worth International Airport, preparing to fly to San Diego where I would preach for five days. Having been on the road preaching and teaching for three consecutive weeks, I was weary. Luckily, because I am a Premier 1K frequent flyer on United Airlines, I received a free upgrade to first class.

I boarded the plane, settled into my seat, and searched the free television shows on the screen in front of me. I also sipped some orange juice, stretched my legs, and looked forward to some rest during the three-hour flight to California.

Once we reached our cruising attitude of thirty-seven thousand feet, the pilot welcomed us and turned off the "Fasten Seat Belts" sign. By this time, I was thoroughly engrossed in a movie and enjoying myself. Suddenly a question came out of nowhere. *Did I lock my car before leaving the airport parking lot?* I became distracted and unsettled.

The question niggled at the back of my mind. I shifted in my seat and asked myself again, *Did* I or *didn't* I lock the car? I couldn't remember hearing the car beep, indicating it had been locked. Before long, I was beating myself up. *How could I have been so foolish and irresponsible? What if someone breaks into my car?*

Though physically I was in the first-class cabin thirty-seven thousand feet in the sky, mentally I was still on the ground, stuck in the DFW airport parking lot with guilt from the past and worry about the future. I was again in two places at once.

STUCK IN THE AIRPORT PARKING LOT

Many of us experience this divisive bilocation. Some of us are here and yet we live in the past, beating ourselves up with guilt for something we did days, months, or even years ago. Kieran lives with the daily guilt that his drinking has destroyed his family. Jason bitterly regrets waiting a day before returning to his mother's bedside; she died early that morning. Marge wishes she could erase last year's act of infidelity. The Chinese say, "Don't let yesterday use up too much of today," but some people allow it to do just that. Guilt drains us emotionally, keeping us morosely self-absorbed and unable to be present to the moment at hand.

Others are like Marc. "I'm a worry wart," he confessed. "I fret over whether I'll have enough money saved for my retirement. I lose sleep over my children and the choices they are making. I stew over tomorrow's staff meeting and agonize, *Do I have everything prepared that my boss wants?*" People like Marc bite their fingernails and obsess over things they cannot control. A Chinese proverb says, "That the birds of worry and care fly over your head, this you cannot change; but that they build nests in your hair, this you can prevent."

A newborn baby, on the other hand, doesn't know the past or future. An infant lives in the present moment. When she is hungry, she cries. When he sees something pleasurable, he smiles. An infant demonstrates that guilt, worry, and anxiety are not natural. These responses are *learned* as we grow up and mature: "Just wait until your father gets home!" teaches the young boy to feel guilty; over-hearing a fretting parent saying, "I'm not sure how we are going to pay the bills this month" exposes a young girl to worry and anxiety. These learned responses keep us on the ground and stuck in the airport parking lot.

> So often people say that we should look to the elderly, learn from their wisdom, their many years. I disagree, I say we should look to the young: untarnished, without stereotypes implanted in their minds, no poison, no hatred in their hearts. When we learn to see life through the eyes of a child, that is when we become truly wise.
>
> Mother Teresa of Calcutta

Jesus insisted we unlearn a lot. He did not want us to be im-prisoned in the past with guilt and regret. So much of his ministry was focused on forgiving and freeing sinners from their past (Matthew 9:6; Luke 7:47; 23:34). Because Jesus did not want us stumbling into tomorrow with worry and anxiety, he urged followers to live in the present moment (Matthew 6:34). His teaching was simple and direct: "Truly I tell you, unless you change and become like children, you will never enter the kingdom of heaven" (Matthew 18:3).

LIVING IN THE PRESENT MOMENT

There's a lot of contemporary chatter on the web, social media, and television about being mindful and living in the present moment. International bestsellers such as Eckhart Tolle's *The Power of Now:*

A Guide to Spiritual Enlightenment cause us to wonder: "What's the big deal? How can this practice be helpful to the Christian disciple?"

The practice of mindfulness is traditionally associated with Buddhism. In that tradition, it refers to the intentional, nonjudgmental awareness of the present moment. It includes attending to the here-and-now and monitoring the thoughts that float down the stream of consciousness. We don't judge those thoughts—we just notice them and let them go. The focus is on ourselves and how our thoughts, sometimes judgmental, shape our understanding and reaction to the present moment. By monitoring our thoughts and their inter-pretations of different situations, we discover how the mind is a source of so much suffering.

For the past fifty years, many medical doctors and psychologists have promoted mindfulness as a technique to achieve a healthy lifestyle. It has been proven to help reduce depression, stress, and addiction. It can increase inner peace.

And it's not just beneficial to our mental and physical health—it's also useful for efficiency and productivity in the workplace. In 2007, Google started offering its employees a seven-week mindfulness meditation course called Search Inside Yourself. Those who have gone through the course speak of being calmer, clear-headed, and more focused.

I'm not a Buddhist. I'm not a medical doctor. I don't work for Google. I'm a committed Christian and a Franciscan priest. I won't argue with the benefits of mindfulness in the Buddhist tradition or according to medical science and the *Harvard Business Review*. Our thoughts and inner dialogue do, in fact, enslave us at times. Mind-fulness techniques do, in fact, help many people live a fuller, more productive life. However, our Christian tradition offers a richer, deeper understanding of the present moment that goes far beyond a cessation of mental suffering, physical ailments, and work distractions. Indeed, it fosters a mystical spirituality that leads to being reborn as a child.

Abandonment to Divine Providence, traditionally ascribed to the late seventeenth, mid-eighteenth century Jesuit Jean-Pierre de Caussade, gives us some insight into the Christian mysticism of the here-and-now. De Caussade calls the present moment a "sacrament." It is holy because it is the portal through which God and angels walk into our lives. Think of the Lord visiting Abraham and receiving hospitality at Abraham's tent in Mamre (Genesis 18:1-33) or Gabriel's visit and invitation to Mary (Luke 1:26-38). To live with attention to the present moment is to be open to a divine visitation.

The story of elderly Simeon also alerts us to this (Luke 2:25-35). Though the elderly are often stereotyped as living in the past with sentimentality, the devout Simeon eagerly lives in the present and waits for a divine promise to be fulfilled: to see the Lord's Messiah. His eyes are wide open and his heart is tight with expectation. When Joseph and Mary bring the newborn Jesus into the temple to perform the customary rituals of the Mosaic law, Spirit-led Simeon's heart breaks wide open and flowers, his eyes twinkle, and he betrays his mindfulness of the present moment with the first words out of his mouth: "Master, now you are dismissing your servant in peace, according to your word" (Luke 2:29). With a mystical vision rooted in the present moment, this righteous man gazes upon the divine.

The prophetess Anna reveals to us another kind of mindfulness, born not of a Spirit-impulse like Simeon's, but from seventy-seven years of grieving in continual temple prayers and fasting (Luke 2:36-38). In a flash, the veil of the ordinary is momentarily lifted and she beholds the Word made flesh in an infant. This moment moves her to break forth in praise as she witnesses the beginning of salvation history's conclusion.

But the present moment is a sacrament for another reason. In de Caussade's words, "Every moment we live through is like an ambassador who declares the will of God." The here-and-now should not be dismissed or ignored because it reveals the divine longings and yearnings in the most ordinary of situations: the outstretched hand of the poor, the cry of the infant, the twinge of conscience to forgive a neighbor, or the Alzheimer's patient needing to be fed. This moment's unmet need or required duty, as Abraham and Mary remind us, affirms and proclaims God's ardent longing and enthusiastic invitation to a deeper relationship with each one of us. If a familial relationship with Jesus is determined by doing the will of God (Matthew 12:50), ordinary mystics are those who attentively respond with childlike wonder to the simple, tedious details of everyday living. "Thy will be done." Mindfulness breeds mysticism.

When he was in charge of the young Jesuits preparing for the priesthood, the future Pope Francis offered them this wise advice: "Do what you are doing and do it well." That's living in the sacrament of the present moment and responding to the will of God.

"DOING THE WILL OF GOD"

I lived with elderly Brother Leon for a number of years. Long retired from his ministry as a bookkeeper for the Franciscan outreach to the poor and needy of Chicago, he spent his days praying, watching television, cleaning the friary kitchen, straightening up our recreation room, and taking care of any other domestic need. He did it all quietly and efficiently. At day's end, when asked how he had spent his day, Leon had a direct and simple reply: "Doing the will of God."

Over the years, he had discovered this moment's unmet need or required duty was the ambassador of the divine will.

> Each minute of life has its peculiar duty—regardless of the appearance that minute may take. The Now-moment is the moment of salvation. Each complaint against it is a defeat; each act of resignation to it is a victory. The moment is always an indication to us of God's will. . . . Nothing is more individually tailored to our spiritual needs than the Now-moment; for that reason it is an occasion of knowledge which can come to no one else. This moment is my school, my textbook, my lesson. . . . To accept the duty of this moment for God is to touch Eternity, to escape from time.
>
> *Fulton J. Sheen*

"But isn't it reckless to live like Brother Leon? As a parent, I need to be sensible. As an employee, I need to be conscientious. Isn't it irresponsible to be attentive to the present moment and neglect the past and future?" you might ask. Yes, it certainly is! But living in the present moment and responding to its unmet need or required duty do not mean ignoring the past and future. Rather, they require us, as Brother Leon reminded me, to be attentive to the sacrament of the present moment as an ambassador—an expression—of God's will right here, right now. If the present moment is asking me to look at the past and balance my checkbook or make an examination of conscience, I do it. If it is asking me to live in the future and plan the menu for next week or discuss my retirement plans with a financial planner, I do it. It's not a matter of choosing between the past, present, or future. It's a matter of being present to where I am and allowing this ambassador to show me where my focus should be—and what God's will is.

"KEEP DEATH BEFORE YOUR EYES"

Ninety-three-year-old Brother David Steindl-Rast, OSB, is an internationally known author, scholar, and Benedictine monk. When Oprah Winfrey interviewed him on *Super Soul Sunday*, he offered a practical way to live in the present moment.

Steindl-Rast grew up in Nazi-occupied Austria and mentioned how, with bombs dropping everywhere, "you are so surprised you are still alive. That forced me to live in the present moment." He continued with a story about one of his teachers giving the class homework due for the following Thursday. "The whole class broke out laughing," Steindl-Rast chuckled. "'*Next Thursday?* Who knows if there'll be a next Thursday?'" The daily possibility of death had taught him and his classmates how to live in the here-and-now.

Out of spite for his Nazi teachers who didn't want the students reading anything spiritual, the future Benedictine monk began reading the Rule of St. Benedict. Discovering Benedict's admonition in chapter four—"Keep death before your eyes at all times"—Steindl-Rast admitted, "That sentence touched me deeply. I realized later on that brought me great joy—to have death before me at all times—because it forced me to live in the present moment."

I mentioned this idea of keeping death before our eyes to Salvador, a spiritual directee, who missed the point. "I don't want to live with an obsession about the morality of every action I perform," he said. "To live with death before my eyes makes me cower with shame, guilt, and self-remorse over my past sins and want to hide in the bushes. It makes me nervous and instills fear over God's future judgment."

Steindl-Rast's own experience and the Benedictine tradition offer another time-tested perspective and interpretation. Living with death in front of us is not meant to inspire fear about the past or distress about the future; it is meant to inspire fascination and delight in this very moment unfolding before us. Like suddenly finding ourselves at a dead end, death jolts us to the present moment and invites us to become aware of where we are right here, right now. From watching the sun set below the horizon to hearing a song that jogs a memory from high school, death inspires—from the Latin *inspirare*, "to breathe or blow into," originally used of a divine being, in the sense "impart a truth or idea to someone"—the celebration of life. It calls us back to the first-class cabin.

A FOUR-STEP METHOD

I was five years old when my mother taught me how to cross the street. "Always remember, Albert," she told me, "when you get to the curb, stop, look, listen—and if you don't see or hear anything—go." Those four simple steps are helpful for living in the present moment and experiencing the mysticism of the mundane. Here's a simple two-minute practice that will bring you back to where you are.

Start by *stopping*. Deliberately call yourself out of the airport parking lot and come back to the first-class cabin. "Re-collect" and gather yourself from all the different places where you are mentally bilocating—whether they be in the past or future.

I remember Catherine telling me her method of recollection. "I intentionally and momentarily pause and close my eyes. I take a few deep breaths. *Cathy,* I ask myself, *where are you?* And I reply, *I'm here, right here.* I open my eyes and briefly look around. Believe it or not, I suddenly find myself right where I am. It works every time."

Once you have returned to the present moment with recollection, *look*. Pay attention to your senses. What are you hearing? Seeing? Feeling? Tasting? Smelling? Your five senses are the keys that open the tabernacle door to the sacrament of the present moment. It's important that you take your time and dally and delight here. Focus on your sense of smell if you're in a flower shop; taste your seafood gumbo; feel the softness of the baby's skin; listen to the coo of the mourning dove; see the desperation on the beggar's face. Fully experience this utterly unique and unrepeatable moment. It will never, ever happen again.

Years ago, I had the opportunity to travel through Western Europe. Flying into Belgium, I slowly snaked my way by train through Germany, Switzerland, Austria, France, and Italy. I was intent on photographing notable landmarks and tourist sites. Upon my return home, I went through the photos and noticed I had seen Bruges's belfry and Halle, Munich's Marienplatz, Vienna's Schönbrunn Palace, the artworks on display in Kunsthaus Zürich, Paris's Eiffel Tower and Arc de Triomphe, and Rome's Colosseum and Trevi Fountain. But as I looked at my photos, I kept wondering, *Was I really there?* I had no memory of being at any of those places. The only vivid memory I had from my European trip was walking the grounds of Dachau concentration camp in silence and horror; I had brought my camera, but once on the grounds of the camp, I realized it was inappropriate to even think about taking photographs.

I learned an important lesson from the trip. Photographs are incapable of replacing what only our five senses can capture: the experience of the now, the sacrament of the present moment.

Having attended to your five senses, briefly *listen.* Reflect upon what your senses are registering. My friend Dennis finds it helpful to ask himself, *What is God saying to me right now? What is God asking me to do?* Momentarily pausing and pondering these two questions might reveal an unmet need or required duty. This third step is letting the present moment be the ambassador that declares God's will.

Being present with full attention is the practice: we do God's will moment by moment, and we surrender wholeheartedly any concern about fruits of action (outcomes). We place ourselves in God's hands and have no inner commentary about how we did and how what we did unfolded. We know not if we will be of any benefit to others or ourselves.

Mary Margaret Funk, OSB

Your recollection (stop), attention (look), and reflection (listen) should blossom into a response. *Go.* The unmet need or required duty might call you to prayer or contemplative silence. It might ask you to share your time, talents, or treasure with someone less fortunate. It might require changing a diaper or resisting the temptation to snap a photograph with your cell phone. It might challenge you to visit a neighbor and offer an apology. The ordinary mystic—like elderly Abram and Sarai as they sat at home (see Genesis 12:1-9), the young Samuel lying in the temple (see 1 Samuel 3:1-9), Matthew at his workplace (see Matthew 9:9-13), the Samaritan woman attending to her household needs (see John 4:1-42), or Zacchaeus in the sycamore tree (see Luke 19:1-10)—is only too aware that God is inviting a response right here, right now.

For those who live with mindfulness, every moment is a divine invitation. By day's end when asked what you did all day, you can reply with Brother Leon's answer, "I did the will of God."

I remember a radio interview when I presented this simple two-minute technique. Someone called in and took exception to it. "Father," the woman asked, "isn't this a bit awkward and contrived?"

I couldn't have agreed more. It *is* artificial and forced. But that awkwardness betrays just how little time we spend right here, right now. We have to make a conscious effort and deliberately return to—or maybe it would be more accurate to say, *arrive at*—where we actually are.

By practicing this two-minute technique a couple of times a day, you'll be on the road to forming a new habit. Gradually that habit will become second nature. Before you know it, you'll surprise yourself by suddenly being right where you are! That's how an adult becomes a child—and an ordinary mystic.

EFFECTS

Craig was driving along the highway when he saw a car parked to the side of the road with its emergency lights blinking and a woman standing beside it. Still feeling the Christmas spirit, Craig made a U-turn, went back, and parked behind the stopped vehicle.

"What's the problem?" he asked.

"I have a flat tire."

Craig looked inside the automobile and saw a man wearing leg braces and a young child in a car seat.

"I think I can help you," he said.

After helping the passengers get out of the car, Craig opened the trunk and went about changing the tire.

Twenty minutes later, the woman thanked him profusely, got back into the car with her passengers, and drove away.

The following day, at Sunday Mass on the Feast of the Holy Family, his thoughts returned to the family he had helped. When the priest casually mentioned, "The Holy Family touches us and comes into our lives in the most ordinary of ways," Craig was dumbfounded. He cocked his head, fought back tears, and asked himself in wonder, *Could they really have been the Holy Family?*

Mindfulness compels us, as it did with Craig, to respond to the unmet need or required duty at hand. That response can lead to wonder and surprise, two childlike qualities delighting the God of disguise. Jesus hinted at this in his parable about the judgment of the nations (see Matthew 25:31-46). The righteous at the right hand of the Son of Man are invited to inherit the kingdom prepared for them: "For I was hungry and you gave me food, I was thirsty and you gave me something to drink, I was a stranger and you welcomed me, I was naked and you gave me clothing, I was sick and you took care of me, I was in prison and you visited me" (Matthew 25:35-36). The righteous are dumbfounded and caught off guard. Fearing the Son of Man was mistaken, they ask in astonishment, "When did we see you hungry, thirsty, a stranger, naked, sick, or in prison?" Highlighting the sacrament of the present moment, the Son of Man responds, "Truly I tell you, just as you did it to one of the least of these who are members of my family, you did it to me" (Matthew 25:40).

Like Craig and the parable's righteous ones, we are not always consciously aware we are standing at the portal to the sacred. Nevertheless, with ardent longing and an enthusiastic invitation to a deeper relationship, God provides this moment's unmet need or required duty as an opportunity for us to get a foothold in the door. Our loving, spontaneous response—be it playful, pragmatic, or proactive—will sometimes unveil a touch of the divine and, in retrospect, awaken surprise, wonder, and awe. These three emotions fuel ordinary mystics.

The spiritual journey challenges us not to feel guilty about the past or anxious about the future; our task is to surrender the past to the mercy of God and to offer the future in trust to God. Our daily pilgrimage is to the first-class cabin called the present moment. Here we experience the extraordinary in the ordinary, as God and angels call us in an unmet need or required duty. There is mysticism in this mundane moment for those who live with mindfulness.

Practice

Spend two minutes experiencing the sacrament and ambassador of the present moment by practicing the four steps: stop, look, listen, go.

What did you discover about God's invitation and will for you right here, right now?

If possible, commit to practicing this exercise three or four times tomorrow. In the evening, assess its usefulness for you.

Reflect

1. How does Brother Leon's understanding of the will of God confirm or challenge your understanding of the will of God?

2. What are some of the common unmet needs or required duties of your daily life? How mindful are you that they are potential portals to the sacred?

Ponder

Mysticism begins with living in the sacrament of the present moment and allowing this ambassador to declare God's will in its unmet need or required duty.

Chapter 2

WHAT'S MISSING?

SELF-AWARENESS SABOTAGES SIN

I recently told a friend about my frustration with the spiritual life. "When I examine my conscience and name the sins I have committed over the past day, week, or month, I notice I commit the same ones over and over. I keep falling into the trap of pride, greed, and selfishness. I get caught in little white lies to protect my reputation. I'm not as generous with my time and money, because I fear there won't be enough left over for me and my needs. And I am so embarrassed by my self-centeredness and fixation on my feelings. You would think, at my age, I would have developed more creative ways to sin!"

My friend offered some homespun wisdom that gave me cause to pause and ponder. He encouraged my self-awareness. "That's half the battle, you know, in overcoming sins. Many people don't practice an examination of conscience. Instead, they live on autopilot with no self-reflection. That's why they default to the same sins over and over again." He then added, "But the real challenge—after you've become mindful of your default sins—is to go deeper and ask yourself *why* you commit those sins. That's when you'll discover what I call cracks in the soul. There's usually one, two, or three of them in each of us. The vast majority of your sins are symptoms of those cracks—sins are often neon arrows pointing to your fundamental weakness, your deficiency, the broken place in the soul. Pondering your sins can lead you to their source. Knowing that crack will give you an added awareness that can be helpful in resisting its sins."

My friend's advice affirmed the importance of mindfulness. Awareness of our default sins and pondering their source can begin our response to God's ardent longing and enthusiastic invitation to a deeper relationship. For the ordinary mystic, mindfulness gives birth to contrition, repentance, and conversion.

CHILDHOOD AND UPBRINGING

I once heard a psychologist talk about the profound effect our childhood and upbringing have on us. She compared the experiences of a newborn child to a building's foundation. Parents pour that foundation for the first ten years, and the finished product often betrays the parents' own experience of childhood with their parents. Highlighting how our early years are dependent on the experiences of our parents, she said, "You would be amazed at how history repeats itself."

Other psychologists, however, note how a person's foundation can shift over time. Acknowledging the importance of our early years, these psychologists caution against the belief that our adult lives are determined by our youth. Since some of us with nourishing upbringings struggle to adjust to a healthy adult life while others, whose early lives were marred by hardship, adjust well to adulthood, nothing is written in stone. As one psychologist writes, "The one with a large foundation and great potential may build a mansion or a hovel, whereas the one with more modest potential may construct a charming cottage."

The experience of love is an important part of a child's foundation. Andrew remembers his parents being aloof and unexpressive of affection. "I thought that was normal. I always felt that attention and love had to be earned. So I was very obedient and worked hard at school. I was sometimes rewarded with a pat on the back from my father or words of encouragement by my mother."

Andrew's experience is a reminder that childhood is a school where we learn about love. Is it offered unconditionally, or does it have to be earned? Conditional love cracks a child's soul and as an adult, the person risks becoming a high achiever vying for the attention, approval, and appreciation of others at any cost.

Yolanda is a confident, vibrant woman in her thirties. "I was raised in a rough Detroit neighborhood," she told me. "But that didn't stop my parents from giving me a wonderful childhood. They were amazing people. My stepfather showered me with praise and gave me the feeling that I could be and do anything despite our modest surroundings. My mother was the disciplinarian; though she would challenge and correct my bad behavior, I never felt criticized. My parents blessed me with a sense of self-acceptance, self-respect, and self-worth."

Were your parents lavish with their praise, or did they hold back? Was criticism often and harsh, thus diminishing your self-acceptance, self-respect, and self-worth? Lack of appreciation and feelings of disapproval make a person's character brittle and sometimes emotionally needy. If this spirals out of control, the adult might be prone to various forms of compulsion or addiction to alleviate the pain of not feeling accepted.

How did the parents respond to their child's hopes and dreams? Negative feedback or outright disregard can sometimes be harmful and cause a person to repress or deny the most ardent desires. This person grows up to become a people pleaser who, like a chameleon, changes color based on the surrounding environment.

Ponder your childhood and upbringing for a moment. What's your initial reaction to them? Do you remember yourself being a happy or sad child? Did you feel loved and affirmed, or do you remember being overlooked and ignored? How have your childhood and upbringing influenced your hopes, dreams, and desires as an adult?

THE EFFECTS OF TRAGEDY

And it's not just parenting that grounds and shapes the child. Traumatic childhood experiences also leave their mark.

Of my four siblings, I was the closest to my father. Our bond went far deeper than the fascination we shared with expensive watches and far beyond the times we spent together in the car as he drove me, an altar boy, to attend daily Mass. Dad was my idol. His loving hug was often a place of refuge and security. In a family where the three boys were taught not to talk about their feelings, I often told him, "I want to be just like you when I grow up."

At age thirteen, I was robbed of my youthful spirit and catapulted into adulthood with my father's death by suicide. That incident not only fractured my soul, but also scarred my personality. I am overly sensitive to the feeling of abandonment and not being invited or included in gatherings. I crave love but initially hesitate to get close to people and make friends for fear they will desert me. Over time I've discovered these personality traits—"cracks in the soul" as my friend calls them—are a direct result of internalizing and personalizing my father's suicide.

> Our spiritual journey does not start with a clean slate. We carry with us a prepackaged set of values and preconceived ideas which, unless confronted and redirected, will soon scuttle our journey, or else turn it into pharisaism, the occupational hazard of religious and spiritual people.
>
> *Thomas Keating*

Our upbringing with its positive and negative experiences shapes the contours of what becomes the adult ego. The late Trappist monk Thomas Keating used to say most of us either lacked or *think* we lacked something in childhood (facts and perception form our reality); consequently, the ego over time develops one or more of four obsessions. These obsessions emerge from the cracks in the soul. Let's take a look at them and see how they are potential sources for our default sins.

EGO OBSESSIONS

Self-concern. Growing up, Melanie lived in three foster homes. She was adopted at age fifteen by a very successful couple who showered her with love. But the memory of being passed around from foster home to foster home had already bored a hole in Melanie's heart. Because she *feels* she wasn't loved enough as a child, she is fixated on herself. Her preoccupation with *self-concern* is apparent in her bold sense of entitlement: she is demanding, often suggesting she deserves better treatment, more authority, and even specific material possessions. Ask her for advice or a favor, and she unabashedly asks, "What's in it for me?"

Melanie's obsession with self-concern keeps her peering over the fence into the lives of others. She struggles with anger and envy, two of the traditional seven deadly sins, as she notices family members and friends who have more material things and are more respected than she. For many people like Melanie, self-concern is the source of their anger and envy.

Self-image. An adult who was an overlooked or underappreciated child could potentially develop an inflated ego. I'm thinking of Clarence, who demands at his workplace what he didn't have in childhood. He is overly concerned about his reputation and what people think of him. His worst fear is looking foolish. This obsession with his *self-image* often explodes into the sins of pride and anger. He pumps more and more hot air into his sense of self-importance by taking personal credit for his gifts and talents and parading his accomplishments before others. He is quick to unleash his anger on anyone who dares to ask, "Just who does Clarence think he is?"

Self-gratification. Some adults think back to their childhoods and can't remember ever being happy. They struggle to see through a thick fog of sorrow or grief. Perhaps the memory of a parent's cruel comment in a moment of frustration stunted their emotional growth, or a neighbor's inappropriate action traumatized them. Any number of childhood experiences can spark an adult obsession with *self-gratification* verbalized in myriad ways: "I want to feel good." "I avoid pain at any cost." "I want to experience the love and esteem of others."

Self-gratification gets a bit risky when it is consistently sought. It becomes the source of three traditional deadly sins: lust, gluttony, and acedia. Learn the backgrounds of those involved in the pornography industry, and you'll discover that sex, a God-given gift to celebrate the love between two people and bring forth life into the world, is commonly used as a medication to mask the pain of some childhood trauma. Gluttony and various forms of compulsive behavior—be it binging on food, alcohol, shopping, or gambling—become a mirage we run toward in hopes of finding relief from unrelenting emotions that we want to avoid and so suppress. Acedia, the deadly sin of ignoring and giving up on God's longing for a deeper relationship, appears enticing when our minimal spiritual progress discourages us and our dull spiritual lives disappoint us.

Self-preservation. Dennis grew up in poverty and a broken home. He remembers Christmases being sparse, with few gifts. His family never ate in a restaurant. "My grammar school classmates were happy-go-lucky, but I found life hard and bitter," he told me during a spiritual direction session. Many of his sins focus on a fourth ego obsession, *self-preservation.* In his preoccupation to have enough food, money, and security—things he lacked as a child—he struggles with selfishness and a self-centered spirit. He is only too aware how the deadly sin of greed shapes his lack of response to the indigent people he encounters on his daily walk from the train station to the office.

LIFE SUPPORT FOR THE SEVEN DEADLY SINS

For most of us, one or more of these four ego obsessions becomes the emotional "operating system" managing our personality. The attempts to satisfy our preoccupation with self-concern, self-image, self-gratification, or self-preservation potentially achieve one of two results. If the attempts are unsuccessful, we become frustrated and unhappy. We wrongly equate happiness with getting a kickback, bolstering our reputation, feeling good, or depositing more money in the bank—in other words, with satisfying our ego obsessions. Think of the rich young man who was unwilling to sell his possessions and went away sad when Jesus challenged his obsession and offered him a path to eternal life (Mark 10:17-22).

If the attempts to satisfy the ego obsession are successful, we are likely to fall into sin. Being creatures of habit who live on autopilot, we tend to choose what has worked in the past. Those choices can become the life support system for the traditional seven deadly sins:

- *Pride* loves to preen before the mirror of self-image.
- *Anger* is preoccupied with self-concern or self-image.
- *Envy* fixates on self-concern.
- *Lust* is passionate about self-gratification.
- *Gluttony* has an appetite for self-gratification and self-preservation.
- *Greed* is anxious over self-preservation.
- *Acedia* is infatuated with self-gratification.

That's why we sometimes commit the same sin or sins over and over. That's the origin of our default sins: they are our vain attempts to appease our ego obsession—and we quickly become mindful of the ego's unquenchable thirst for satisfaction.

AN EXAMINATION OF CONSCIENCE

> We need [discernment] at all times, to help us recognize God's timetable, lest we fail to heed the promptings of his grace and disregard his invitation to grow. . . . For this reason, I ask all Christians not to omit, in dialogue with the Lord, a sincere daily "examination of conscience."
>
> Pope Francis

Because many people live on autopilot and sleepwalk their way through the present moment, they might be aware of the sins they commonly commit—their default sins—but don't know *why* they commit them. That was my experience when I talked with my friend. A spiritual practice that helps to turn off autopilot and to foster mindful self-awareness is the examination of conscience. It is helpful for any ordinary mystic burdened by the weight of recurring sins.

There are many ways to practice an examination of conscience. Reflect upon the Ten Commandments and with each one, ask yourself,

- *How well do I respect this commandment on a daily basis?*
- *When and why am I tempted to break it?*
- *How often have I broken it?*

Another examination of conscience is based upon the Beatitudes. As you read each, found in Matthew 5:3-12, ask yourself,

- *How do I witness to this Beatitude in my daily life?*
- *How and why does it challenge my current lifestyle?*
- *What thoughts, words, and deeds can strengthen my expression of this Beatitude?*

Here's a third examination of conscience. It's a bit daunting and requires about an hour to complete. It's based on the seven deadly sins and an ordinary mystic's three essential relationships: God, others, and oneself.

Spend a few minutes breathing deeply and gathering your thoughts. Come back to the present moment. Spend ample time surveying and reflecting on your thoughts, words, and actions over the past couple of months.

You might find it helpful to draw a large pie on a blank piece of paper. Divide the pie into three slices and label them "God," "Others," "Me."

Relationship with God. As you ponder the slice labeled "God," ask yourself the following questions.

- PRIDE: When have I taken personal credit for my God-given gifts and talents? How have I refused to acknowledge my absolute dependence on God? *Why?*
- ANGER: When have I refused to express my disappointment or despair to God? How have I hidden uncomfortable emotions from God? *Why* do I think some feelings are inappropriate to bring before God?
- ENVY: When have I given more importance to what others have—be it power, prestige, or possessions—and not acknowledged in gratitude what God has given me? *Why* do I want more, and *why* am I dissatisfied with what God has given me?
- LUST: How have I misused or been unaccepting of God's gift of my sexuality? *Why?*
- GLUTTONY: How have I expected material things—food, drink, drugs, clothes, gaming—to satisfy what only God can satisfy? *Why* do I choose such things?
- GREED: How have my attitudes and actions betrayed my fear that God would not provide for me? *Why* do I allow those attitudes and actions to persist?
- ACEDIA: How and when have I allowed disappointment and discouragement in my spiritual life to affect my time in prayer? How often have I not taken time for God or refused to acknowledge God's invitation to a deeper relationship? *Why?*

As you reflect upon the final "Why?" after each sin, consider writing in the slice any insights you discover about your relationship with God.

Relationship with others. As you ponder the slice labeled "Others," ask yourself the following questions.

- PRIDE: When have I reminded someone just how important I think I am? How often have I used my accomplishments and feelings of superiority to belittle other people? *Why* do I need to feel more important than others?

- ANGER: When has my harsh response to others moved them to tears? How often have I felt the need to punish someone with a tongue lashing? *Why* do I often use anger as my response to situations?

- ENVY: How often have I felt envious of another's accomplishments or possessions? When have I felt jealous of another's relationships? *Why* do I need to compare myself to others?

- LUST: When have I looked at or used others as an object of my own personal satisfaction? How have my actions supported the pornography industry? *Why* is the inappropriate expression of my sexual desires an issue with me?

- GLUTTONY: When have I allowed myself to be seduced by the advertising industry, television commercials, and social media advertisements? *Why* is it important for me to have more and more?

- GREED: How often have I refused to share my time, talents, or treasures with those in need? When did I ignore the outstretched hand or unmet need of the moment? *Why* do I refuse to share what I have with others?

- ACEDIA: When did I refuse to strengthen the relationships with my closest family and friends? How often have my actions and attitudes toward others been dismissive of those I love most dearly? *Why* do I hesitate to show my love and affection?

As you reflect upon the final "Why?" after each sin, consider writing in the slice any insights you discover about your relationship with others.

Relationship with self. As you ponder the slice labeled "Me," ask yourself the following questions.

- PRIDE: When did I show an unhealthy self-respect? How do I allow my lack or abundance of self-esteem to affect my attitudes and actions? *Why* are self-respect and self-esteem so important to me?
- ANGER: When did I allow anger and frustration to seethe within me? How often did I inappropriately express anger? *Why* do I feel it is always important to conceal or express it?
- ENVY: How often did I feel I didn't have enough and wanted more? *Why* are material possessions so important for me?
- LUST: When did I disrespect my body? How often did I allow my sexual impulses to control my attitudes and actions? *Why* do I give free rein to my sexual desires?
- GLUTTONY: How often did I binge with food, drink, shopping, or gaming? When did I say to myself, "I went too far"? *Why* am I driven to overindulge?
- GREED: When did I cling to something I could have shared? How often did I find myself hoarding? *Why* do I feel the need to hold tightly to some things?
- ACEDIA: How often did I allow discouragement and disillusionment to affect my attitudes and actions? When did I give up on a commitment or promise? *Why* do I let despair and melancholy influence my attitudes and actions?

As you reflect upon the final "Why?" after each sin, consider writing in the slice any insights you discover about your relationship with yourself.

THE UNRELENTING "WHY?"

You probably noticed that each sin's examination ended with a "Why?" Spending ample time formulating an answer is critical to discerning which of the four ego obsessions are controlling your life. But unmasking the obsession is easier said than done. It's rarely exposed in one session of an examination of conscience. The ego is highly protective of itself, easily threatened, and justifies its obsession with layer upon layer of rationalizations. You must be patient as you peel away and challenge the rationalizations with brutal self-honesty and objectivity.

If you are having difficulty answering the "Why?" question or uncovering your ego obsession, it might be helpful to ask, "What did I lack or *think* I lacked in my childhood?" That often leads to the cracks in your soul that shape the ego. Because the ego smarts when exposed, you know you are getting close to naming the obsession when your answer to the question begins to make you squirm or causes you embarrassment.

It took me more than eight months of practicing that examination of conscience on a monthly basis before my ego obsessions became manifestly clear. The delay was caused by thick layers of excuses that protected my ego; it took time to get underneath them. But once I was willing to be honest with myself and admit how flimsy my rationalizations were, I saw time and again how an excessive concern for self-image and self-preservation were the sources for my recurring, default sins of pride and greed. Not surprisingly, they grew out of the experience of personalizing my father's suicide at the beginning of my adolescence. Being the child closest to my father, I felt he must have been disappointed in me, thereby contributing to his death. The financial difficulties caused by his death certainly contributed to my excessive preoccupation never to "be without." Ironically, I joined a religious community known for its poverty and yet, deep down inside, part of my attraction to the Franciscans was the security of bed and board it offered; joining the friars was a way to ensure a sense of well-being and the confidence of self-preservation that were missing from the end of my childhood.

Being mindful of my ego obsessions hasn't stopped me from putting myself on a pedestal or being greedy at times. Human nature is weak, lifelong habits are hard to break, and the spiritual journey is endless. I'm not discouraged—actually, I am encouraged. Awareness of my ego obsessions urges me to respond yet again to God's ardent longing and enthusiastic invitation to a deeper relationship. The deeper my response, the more magnified the awareness of my sinfulness. That's why saints and mystics often think of themselves as the worst of sinners. In his first encounter with Jesus, Peter did not hesitate to say, "Go away from me, Lord, for I am a sinful man!" (Luke 5:8). And Jesus's response? "Do not be afraid" (Luke 5:10). Mindfulness of sin nurtures a response to this present moment, glistening with grace. It's part of the journey to becoming an ordinary mystic.

Practice

Spend one hour practicing the examination of conscience with its unrelenting "Why?" Afterward, assess its usefulness in helping you name your recurring sins and the ego obsession to which each points.

Reflect

1. With which of the traditional seven deadly sins (pride, anger, envy, lust, greed, gluttony, acedia) do you most struggle? Consider how it might be related to a real or perceived childhood deficiency.

2. What feelings arise when you reflect on your sinfulness? How do you respond to those feelings? What might God be asking of you in those feelings?

Ponder

Ordinary mystics are encouraged by the awareness of their sins.

Chapter 3

JESUS THE ELECTRICIAN

THE PRACTICAL MYSTICISM
OF THE SERMON ON THE MOUNT

The title of the evening presentation, "A Rabbi, a Minister, and a Priest Walk into a Bar and Reflect upon the Sermon on the Mount," sounded like the beginning of a joke. However, the three presentations left the audience mesmerized with more than forty-five minutes' worth of questions, comments, and reactions. I appreciated the unique insights of each presenter.

The rabbi noted the detail of Jesus sitting down before he began his teaching. "Jesus is portraying himself as a teacher who gathers and instructs his students," the rabbi said. He noted Jesus' clever use of blessings, pithy sayings, and even exaggeration—"He teaches in a manner any first-century Jew would find intriguing. And maybe even a bit scandalous when he disregards the Torah by saying, 'You have heard it said . . . But I say to you . . .'" The rabbi suggested Jesus taught in the tradition of the great prophets like Isaiah and

Jeremiah, calling his audience to radical, ethical, and virtuous living. The audience chuckled when the rabbi feigned a thick Yiddish accent and concluded, "Oy vey! Good luck trying to put the Sermon on the Mount into practice!"

The evangelical minister highlighted the difficult ethical challenges mentioned in the Sermon. "It's impossible to live what Jesus is asking us—never lusting or hating; following the way of nonviolence that requires turning the other cheek; living worry-free and never judging others. It's all impossible! We're all sinners." The minister imitated the rabbi by concluding, "Oy vey! That's why we need the grace of God and the righteousness Jesus won for us on the cross."

The priest talked about Jesus as the New Lawgiver and the Sermon on the Mount as the New Law. "With punchy, vivid, and direct metaphors, Jesus is not simply rocking the boat but is boldly declaring war on the values of this world," he said, talking off-text. "Of the five major discourses found in Matthew, the Sermon on the Mount is the foundation of everything else found in the first gospel." After speaking for thirty minutes on the Beatitudes and select passages from the Sermon on the Mount, the priest concluded by quoting a Lutheran biblical scholar who said, "Jesus doesn't preach the Sermon on the Mount to make his followers feel guilty—but to offer signs and symptoms of what happens when grace seizes a child of God."

Listening to the three presentations gave me a deeper appreciation for the different ways the Sermon on the Mount has been interpreted. The rabbi gave me an appreciation for the Sermon's Jewishness, the minister for its challenge, and the priest for its fruits.

THE REAL SOURCE OF HAPPINESS

Matthew's Sermon on the Mount (Matthew 5–7) parallels Luke's Sermon on the Plain (Luke 6:20-49). Matthew's text is longer

than Luke's and contains sayings of Jesus that are topically arranged. More than a mere compendium of Jesus' teachings, the
Sermon on the Mount can be interpreted in still another way:
as an incisive critique of how we understand happiness and the
good life.

> The emphasis in Jesus' ministry on repentance means "change the
> direction in which you are looking for happiness."
>
> *Thomas Keating*

We are hardwired for happiness. For most of us, that happiness
is found in satisfying the four ego obsessions that operate and manage
our lives in one way or another: self-concern, self-image, self-
gratification, or self-preservation. Whatever our obsession, happiness
means its satisfaction. As we saw in the previous chapter, that
obsession doesn't appear out of nowhere—it has its roots in our
desire to acquire what we lacked or *think* we lacked in our childhood.
Being mindful of the deficiency of our upbringing is one way to
open ourselves to the present moment where God invites us to a
deeper relationship, to repentance and conversion.

Here's another way of saying it: the thoughts that consume us
on a daily basis are shaping our response to God and our spiritual
life. That's because our thoughts awaken desires—and those desires
either strengthen the ego or pull the plug on its life support system
(the obsessions). When we live on autopilot, without mindfulness
of our thoughts, desires, and childhood deficiency, we tend to act
impulsively on our ego obsessions—that's why we commit those
recurring, default sins. It's a chain reaction: Thoughts awaken desires
that can strengthen the ego's grip on us. When we act upon those
ego desires—"sin"—we're fortifying the ego and deceiving ourselves
into thinking we have found happiness.

Let me give you an example from my own life. I like to think of myself as intelligent and gifted. *I have a doctorate. I've become somewhat successful as a writer. I have a natural gift for preaching.* Those thoughts awaken the desire to be treated with respect and admiration. And that desire feeds the obsession with my self-image. If you slight me with disrespect, I'll respond in anger. The angry word I bark at you had its origin, not in your disrespect, but in what I was thinking. My thought, the desire for the esteem of others it gave birth to, and the subsequent anger that arose when the desire was unmet, affected both my response to you and to God's invitation to a deeper relationship at that very moment.

Another way to avoid recurring sins, besides awareness of my ego obsessions with their source in a real or perceived childhood deficiency, is by deliberately pulling the plug on the ego's desires. To do that, we need to change our thinking about what happiness and the good life are. This presents another interpretation of the Sermon on the Mount.

PRACTICAL MYSTICISM

Like a master electrician, Jesus is rewiring our thinking about what it means to be blessed and happy. (The Greek word *makarios*, usually translated as "blessed," can also mean "happy" or "fortunate.") His understanding, requiring a vision focused on the kingdom, is both countercultural and mystical. And yet, it is also eminently practical and ordinary—Jesus systematically pulls the plug not only on the four ego obsessions but also on the desires and thoughts feeding them. Beginning with his Beatitudes (Matthew 6:3-12), Jesus offers an enthusiastic invitation to think in a new way and change the direction in which we are looking for happiness.

- He replaces a preoccupation with *self-preservation* with the fortunes of being poor in spirit;
- a fixation on *self-gratification* with the joys of having desires disappointed and hopes dashed ("Blessed are they who mourn");
- an appetite for *self-concern* with hungering for conduct in conformity with God's, not our own, will (what Matthew calls "righteousness");
- an obsession with *self-image* with being meek, merciful, persecuted, and insulted.

It's clear, as St. Paul states, that we need to "be transformed by the renewing of your minds" (Romans 12:2). By changing how we think about the ego obsessions, adopting the mindset of the Beatitudes, and looking in a different direction for happiness, we can change our behavior—are "transformed"—and end the cycle of recurring sin.

This requires mindfulness: not simply the awareness of how the ego obsessions are managing our lives, but mindfulness of our thoughts. Because thoughts affect our spiritual life, by acknowledging our ego-centered thoughts and replacing them with Jesus'—"Let the same mind be in you that was in Christ Jesus" (Philippians 2:5)—we become ordinary mystics.

Continuing in the Sermon on the Mount, Jesus scorns thoughts of self-concern or self-absorption.

- If we go to worship and remember a neighbor who bears a grudge against us, we should forget the self and seek forgiveness immediately (Matthew 5:23-26).
- Jesus challenges us to turn the other cheek and make generosity and charity the response to any unmet need, required duty, inconvenience, or trial (Matthew 5:39-41).

- Jesus erases any battle lines drawn in the sand by telling us to love
  and pray for the enemy and not to judge (Matthew 5:44, 7:1-5).

When I am tempted to bolster my self-image with proud or
arrogant thoughts, I need to remind myself that Jesus teaches I am
"salt." Mixing metaphors, he says the light of my good works is for
the glory of God, not myself (Matthew 5:13-16). Jesus rewires my
conceited and snobbish thinking using the expression, "You have
heard that it was said . . . But I say to you," insisting that anger makes
me liable for judgment (Matthew 5:21-22) and forbidding me from
polishing my reputation with showy acts of piety (Matthew 6:1-18).

For those who have a hankering for VIP treatment, he levels the
playing field by stating explicitly: "In everything do to others as you
would have them do to you; for this is the law and the prophets"
(Matthew 7:12). He directly confronts any sense of spiritual entitlement based on one's actions, and clearly points those who want
to enter into the kingdom to the will of God (Matthew 7:21-23).

Jesus attacks a preoccupation with self-gratification by revealing
the challenging terrain where the narrow gate leading to eternal life
is found (Matthew 7:13-14).

- He internalizes the prohibition against adultery, broadening it
  to include thoughts and desires; with hyperbolic and exag-
  gerated commands, he highlights how the senses can lead to sin
  (Matthew 5:27-30).

- He does not allow retaliation for injury, and replaces it with a
  spirit of nonviolence (Matthew 5:38-39).

- He forbids spiritual arrogance, vanity, materialism, and a lifestyle based upon the demands of a consumeristic society: "No
  one can serve two masters . . . You cannot serve God and
  wealth" (Matthew 6:1-18, 19-21, 24).

> Eventually we reach a point in the spiritual life where, precisely
> because we are proficient at being good and decent, we are
> invited, like the rich young man in the gospels, to give up our
> most-cherished comforts and securities and plunge into the
> unknown in a radically new way.
>
> *Ronald Rolheiser*

Jesus contests the belief that happiness is found in self-preservation
and feelings of security. In one of the most beloved passages of the
Gospels, he chastises our worry and anxiety about tomorrow as he
instills within us a mystic's confidence in God's providence: "Look at
the birds of the air. . . . Consider the lilies of the field" (Matthew 6:25-34).
Live mindfully in the sacrament of the present moment.

THINKING WITH THE SERMON ON THE MOUNT

Mindfulness of our thoughts and desires doesn't happen by osmosis.
It needs to be deliberately developed and intentionally practiced.
Here's a practical way to rewire our thinking and to put on the mind
of Christ.

1. Become aware of the ego obsessions operating in your life. It
   might be helpful to revisit the examination of conscience in the
   previous chapter or to ask yourself, "What did I lack or *think* I
   lacked in my childhood?" to bring it to conscious awareness.

2. Reflect on the thoughts associated with those ego obsessions.
   How and in what situations do they manifest themselves to you?

3. What desires are born from those ego-obsessed thoughts?

4. When you find yourself in a situation where those thoughts and
   desires manifest themselves, stop. Take a few deep breaths and
   come back to the present moment. Deliberately say to yourself,
   Following this thought or fulfilling its desire will not make me happy.

It's a passing temptation. I will strive first for the kingdom of God and his righteousness (see Matthew 6:33).

5. Psychologists tell us that ninety consecutive choices form a habit—"Oy vey," to quote the Jewish rabbi. By gradually and consecutively refusing to feed the ego obsession and by replacing its originating thought and subsequent desire with Jesus' wisdom, we grow in the freedom of an ordinary mystic.

A spiritual directee tells me he struggles with viewing inappropriate internet sites. He's stressed out at work and typically comes home late, after his wife and child have gone to bed. Once home, he usually heads straight to the computer, turns it on, and views some internet sites "as a way to clear my mind, relax, and forget my work." He does it all on autopilot, out of habit, without reflection. But after learning about mindfulness and the usefulness of monitoring his thoughts and actions, he's beginning to respond differently. He literally stops as he walks to the computer. He takes a few deep breaths and comes back to the here-and-now. *Charlie,* he says to himself, *this is not going to make you happy. It won't last. Choose a response befitting the kingdom of God.* He still fails on occasion—habits are hard to break as we all know. But on many evenings, his mindfulness helps him respond to God's ardent longing and enthusiastic invitation to a deeper relationship. Charlie's becoming an ordinary mystic.

Short in stature, Beth has always believed the only way she would get the attention and recognition she never had but craves, is to bully her way through every hour of the workday. In a staff meeting, she's beginning to think that no one is listening to her advice. The need to intimidate her colleagues suddenly rears its head. But she's aware of it and chooses not to act on it. *It's not going to make me happy. Blessed are the meek.* After the meeting, as she walks back to her office, she says a prayer of gratitude to God for giving her the grace to kill to her ego.

The Sermon on the Mount skillfully challenges and changes the way we think about happiness and success. It reminds us with very practical advice that the Christian life is countercultural: the Sermon stresses humility, dependence on God, love, forgiveness, peace, simplicity, and the Golden Rule—all fruits of responding to the unmet need or required duty of the present moment that pull the plug on the ego with its demanding obsessions. Consequently, we discover the Sermon on the Mount as both the light for an alternative life of happiness and the pedestrian path to practical mysticism.

Practice

Review the five-step technique for thinking with the Sermon on the Mount. Try practicing it tomorrow with a sin you typically commit while on autopilot.

Assess the technique's helpfulness to you after you have completed it.

Reflect

1. How do you interpret the Sermon on the Mount (Matthew 5–7)? What thoughts and feelings arise when you reflect upon it?

2. What thoughts and desires of yours have to change for you to become more Christlike? How can you respond to God's grace to facilitate that transformation?

Ponder

In the Sermon on the Mount, Jesus is like a master electrician who rewires our thinking and offers us an alternative way to think about happiness.

Chapter 4

CARDIAC SPIRITUALITY

THE FRUIT OF MYSTICISM

What has God been doing with you this past month, Cynthia?" I asked after we had settled into our chairs to begin a spiritual direction session.

Cynthia's face betrayed her unease.

"Not much, Father," she replied. "As a matter of fact, as I look back not only on the past month but also this past year, I realize I haven't made much spiritual progress. I sit down to pray and am riddled with distractions. I have trouble concentrating on a Scripture passage. I continue struggling to understand certain doctrines of our faith like the Trinity. I think I can count on two fingers the number of times I remember feeling the presence of God. I don't find my Sunday church attendance particularly uplifting or helpful to my spiritual growth—it's boring. To tell you the truth, I wonder if God has decided that his grace can be put to better use on someone else." Cynthia paused with embarrassment and fatigue.

"How's your relationship with your husband and kids?" I asked.

"Oh, they really are the light of my life. You know that—I've said it time and time again. I am so grateful to God for bringing Brian into my life and blessing us with Alison and Eileen. I just love them to death."

"Are you aware that those three people along with your extended family, friends, coworkers, and even strangers are an arena in which your spiritual life gets played out? And that God conveys an ardent longing and enthusiastic invitation to a deeper relationship through them?" I asked.

Puzzled, Cynthia cocked her head. "I'm not sure what you mean. I thought the spiritual life was about prayer, fasting, and almsgiving."

"I mean, God's grace is experienced *in* relationships." I continued, "Your spiritual formation occurs in the daily joys and struggles of all your relationships. Prayer and church attendance are important—don't get me wrong, those are two ways to build a relationship with God—but your *relationships* are also a major component of your spiritual life. That's where God's love for you—that ardent divine longing—takes on flesh, and that's where you respond in love to God's enthusiastic invitation. The spiritual life is ultimately about love."

I'm not sure Cynthia was convinced. Like many people, she thought her spiritual life was more about her spirit and less about her life.

AN OLD MISCONCEPTION

Many of us live dualistic lives. We believe there is a wall dividing the secular—"what's down here"—from the sacred—"what's up there." We equate the secular with the mundane, nitty-gritty details of our daily life: earning a living, raising a family, getting the car's oil changed, cutting the grass, and doing the dishes. "It's all about the drudgery of what happens between birth and death," a college student once told me.

And then there is the realm of the sacred. This specifically refers to "religious" activities such as saying prayers, performing pious actions, and obeying the Ten Commandments. Such spiritual practices keep us connected with "what's up there." Consequently, we measure our spiritual growth by the perceived quality of our prayer lives, our felt experiences of God, the number of Scripture passages we have memorized, and the times we resisted temptation. This simplistic reduction of the spiritual to the superficial and external makes it easy for us to think we are maturing in the spiritual life.

That was the oasis the Pharisees provided for the spiritually thirsty of their day. The Pharisees were pious Jews who developed a rule-oriented spirituality based upon the Torah and its oral interpretation. They wanted to refresh a person's soul through obedience to dos and don'ts. The tithing of herbs (Matthew 23:23; Luke 11:42), the wearing of conspicuous phylacteries and tassels (Matthew 23:5), the keen attention to ritual purity (Mark 7:1-4), fasting (Matthew 9:14), and meticulous distinctions in oaths (Matthew 23:16-18) were all practices the Pharisees hoped would offer solace and a sacred connection for the weary people of their day.

The Pharisees were right in thinking that spirituality had to be expressed in a person's life; it can't be compartmentalized. The problem was . . . their strategy didn't work. Their oasis was a mirage. Their promoted spiritual practices became fixations that didn't seep below the surface of the skin; they were merely external and cosmetic. Spirituality was reduced to rigid legalism (see Jesus' criticism in Matthew 23:13–28) and its spiritual practices became "heavy burdens" placed on people's shoulders (Matthew 23:4).

The cosmetic spirituality of the Pharisees continues to this very day. Years ago, I met a young priest ordained for three years. Parishioners referred to him behind his back as "Father Jot-and-Tittle." He fixated on paperwork, policy, and procedures—and forgot about people. He meticulously focused on the least significant aspects of liturgical rubrics or the most insignificant facet of a required action and, as a result, lost the perspective of the bigger picture. His celebration of any of the sacraments devolved into a robotic travesty that hardly led the participants into an encounter with God. "God likes it done perfectly," he proudly confided in me. Sadly, his obsessive preoccupation with detail verged on scrupulosity and sometimes kept him awake at night.

A NEW COMMANDMENT

Brother Pat came to the Franciscan Order as a civil lawyer with licenses to practice in his home state of Wisconsin as well as Ohio and Illinois. Though he never felt called to priestly ordination, after his profession of lifelong vows in the Order, he continued his studies to become a canon lawyer in the Catholic Church. He quickly gained the reputation as an expert in the law of the church and became a regular speaker at the annual meeting of the Canon Law Society of America.

Knowing his reputation, I presumed he would be a stickler regarding legal matters of the church. In need of some advice about a sensitive issue regarding a couple who had presented themselves for marriage, I telephoned him.

Having told him about my case and dilemma, he replied with a compassion that caught me off guard. "The purpose of church law is not to bind and constrict people," he said. "Its purpose is to free people to love and to experience God in new and surprising ways.

That's why Jesus sometimes violated the law. He healed on the Sabbath—which was forbidden in his day—and didn't always obey the dietary laws that guaranteed ritual purity. Though I could never say this as a civil lawyer, as a canon lawyer I can: sometimes the law must give way to love, mercy, and compassion. That's why I always say, if you want to interpret church law correctly, you must have the cardiac spirituality of Jesus."

"*The cardiac spirituality of Jesus?* What do you mean?"

He replied, "Love comes before the law. Love infuses the law. Love is the fulfillment of the law."

Brother Pat's expression, "cardiac spirituality," has stuck with me over the years. It captures Jesus' understanding of the law, the spiritual life, and even mysticism. Unlike the Pharisees, neither of Jesus' understandings—of Sabbath keeping or dietary restrictions—was hooked to a superficial, obedience-based piety. Knowing such an emphasis on externals only scorches the surface and sparks fanaticism, not fire, Jesus pointed to the heart as the source of a person's actions: "Do you not see that whatever goes into the mouth enters the stomach, and goes out into the sewer? But what comes out of the mouth proceeds from the heart, and this is what defiles. For out of the heart come evil intentions, murder, adultery, fornication, theft, false witness, slander. These are what defile a person, but to eat with unwashed hands does not defile" (Matthew 15:17-20). Jesus's cardiac spirituality was about developing and acting from a loving, merciful, and compassionate heart—not an obsessively obedient one.

Love raged and crackled in Jesus' heart. Its sparks shot into the lives of marginalized women and children, public sinners, and outcasts of his day. It stoked his parables about mercy and compassion as well as his teachings in the Sermon on the Mount about stopping the cycle of violence and turning the other cheek, doing good to one's enemies, and forgiving without limitations. It blazed in his final act of laying down his life for his friends and enemies.

Once for all, then, a brief precept is given to you: Love, and do what you want. If you are silent, be silent with love; if you cry out, cry out with love; if you chastise, chastise with love; if you spare, spare with love. The root of love must be within; nothing but good can come forth from this root.

Augustine of Hippo

Jesus ignited this fire in his disciples. Summarizing the Torah and prophets in the command to love God and neighbor (see Matthew 22:34-40), he passed it on as a torch to the next generation: "I give you a new commandment, that you love one another. Just as I have loved you, you also should love one another. By this everyone will know that you are my disciples, if you have love for one another" (John 13:34-35). Jesus' cardiac spirituality includes being mindful of this present moment's unmet need or required duty and responding to it with a loving, merciful, humble, and compassionate heart. It is surrender: "Not my will but yours be done" (Luke 22:42). It is sacrifice: "No one takes [my life] from me, but I lay it down of my own accord" (John 10:18). It is service: "For the Son of Man came not to be served but to serve, and to give his life a ransom for many" (Mark 10:45).

Paul highlights the inability of any cosmetic or Pharisaical spirituality to offer light or assistance on the spiritual journey. In one of his most beloved passages, he writes to the church of Corinth, "If I speak in the tongues of mortals and of angels, but do not have love, I am a noisy gong or a clanging cymbal. And if I have prophetic powers, and understand all mysteries and all knowledge, and if I have all faith, so as to remove mountains, but do not have love, I am nothing. If I give away all my possessions, and if I hand over my body so that I may boast, but do not have love, I gain nothing" (1 Corinthians 13:1-3). In similar fashion, Thomas Merton points out the potential danger of a rule-based spirituality: "Love in fact *is* the spiritual life, and without it all the other exercises of the spirit, however lofty, are emptied of content and become mere illusions. The more lofty they are, the more dangerous the illusion."

LOVE'S INTEGRATION

The First Letter of John tears down any possible wall separating the secular from the sacred by bluntly equating Jesus's cardiac spirituality with a rebirth: "Beloved, let us love one another, because love is from God; everyone who loves is born of God and knows God. Whoever does not love does not know God, for God is love" (1 John 4:7-8). This love-based spirituality is so tightly integrated with godly enthusiasm that John calls those who hate their neighbor yet claim to love God "liars" (1 John 4:20). Secular and sacred are intertwined in his mystical approach, "for those who do not love a brother or sister whom they have seen, cannot love God whom they have not seen" (1 John 4:20). He cogently summarizes his point by stating, "The commandment we have from him is this: those who love God must love their brothers and sisters also" (1 John 4:21). Without Jesus' torch of love, we stagger in darkness, the blind leading the blind.

> The most certain sign, in my opinion, as to whether or not we are observing [love of God and love of neighbor] is whether we observe well the love of neighbor. . . . The more advanced you see you are in love for your neighbor the more advanced you will be in the love of God. . . . I cannot doubt this.
>
> *Teresa of Avila*

The integration of love of God and neighbor is no more evident than in the life of the Secular Franciscan and ordinary mystic, Julia Greeley. Born into slavery sometime between 1833 and 1848 in Hannibal, Missouri, she lost her right eye when a slave owner, while beating her mother, caught it with his whip. Freed by the state's Emancipation Act of 1865, Julia earned a living as a housekeeper and nanny to white families in Missouri, Wyoming, New Mexico, and Colorado. Baptized a Roman Catholic in 1880 at Sacred Heart Church in Denver, she quickly developed a strong devotion to the Sacred Heart of Jesus. This devotion fueled her love for the poor and firefighters. Known as Denver's "Angel of Mercy" and once referred to as a "one-person St. Vincent de Paul Society," Julia, with crippling arthritis, would spend her nights pulling a little red wagon filled with clothes and food through dark alleys. She distributed these necessities to the needy. She often did her acts of charity in secret and always under cover of night, so people wouldn't suffer the embarrassment of being helped by a black woman. When her ten-dollar monthly salary ran out, she would beg for the poor. She expressed her compassion for firefighters who faced multiple dangers from poorly constructed buildings in the nineteenth century by traveling on foot every month to every Denver firehouse where she delivered devotional materials to Catholics and non-Catholics alike. Julia Greeley died on June 7, 1918, the feast of the Sacred Heart of Jesus, and more than a thousand people attended her funeral. Her Cause for Canonization was officially opened in December 2016, because Christians see in the loving heart of this ordinary mystic the merger of the secular with the sacred.

THE DECISION TO LOVE

Julia Greeley and others like her remind us that the present moment is an ambassador declaring God's will in the unmet need or required duty before us. Having the mind of Christ taught in the Sermon on the Mount and responding to this moment with Jesus' cardiac spirituality of love—surrender, sacrifice, and service—are the definitive indications of spiritual growth. This integration of Christ's two-fold love command is ordinary mysticism.

Such love, however, is sorely misunderstood. Many believe it to be an emotion like infatuation or romantic love, but how can we have such feelings for strangers whose names we don't even know? A Chinese atheist gave me an insight.

Zhang Wen, my colleague at the Chinese university in Beijing where I was teaching, invited me to be the honored guest at her twenty-fifth wedding anniversary banquet. I was seated at the table with her, her husband, and their elderly parents.

Though I always spoke with Zhang Wen in English, I wanted to include everyone at the table in our conversation. So in the course of the meal, I asked in broken, halting Chinese, "*Nǐ shénme shíhòu fāxiàn nǐ yǐjīng zhuì rù àihé* [When did you discover you had fallen in love]?"

There was an awkward silence. And then everyone spontaneously burst out laughing. Embarrassed and red-faced, I feigned laughter.

With a smile the size of the Great Wall, Zhang Wen looked at me and jokingly said, "*Nǐ fēngle* [You've lost your mind]!" She then continued in her impeccable English, "Albert, that's one of the big cultural differences between Chinese and Westerners. You Westerners make lifetime decisions based upon feelings and emotions. And so you marry for love. You don't seem to realize that emotions are like the weather that rolls into your life and rolls out.

"For my generation of Chinese, marriage is not based on emotions. It's an act of the will, a decision. Two people decide to share a life, a bank account, and a bed. It is not based on an emotion but on commitment."

I was taken aback by such a facile explanation of one of life's most important decisions. But as I thought about it over the days that followed, I gained an insight into Jesus' cardiac spirituality.

We certainly can't have emotional feelings of love and affection for everyone, especially the people we do not know. It's difficult to feel fondness for those who betray us or whom we consider the enemy. But Christian love is not based on feelings and emotions. It's an unswerving commitment to never refuse forgiveness; a firm resolve to keep my heart opened to everyone regardless of race, color, or creed; and, as exemplified in the life of Julia Greeley, a faithful dedication to help those in need. It is the decision to be intentionally selfless for the sake of others: surrender, sacrifice, and service. It is the spirit of liberal and lavish hospitality that sparkles in the lives of ordinary mystics. Christian love is living the Golden Rule for the common good: "In everything do to others as you would have them do to you; for this is the law and the prophets" (Matthew 7:12). As Paul reminded the Christians in Rome, "Love does no wrong to a neighbor; therefore, love is the fulfilling of the law" (Romans 13:10). He aptly advised the Corinthians, "Let all that you do be done in love" (1 Corinthians 16:14).

THE WORKS OF MERCY

When evening comes, you will be examined in love.

John of the Cross

Christian tradition has given birth to the practice of the works of mercy inspired by Matthew 25:31-46. It has numbered these works as seven. Though considered literal actions, their metaphorical interpretation gives us insight into the decision to love that blazes in the cardiac spirituality of the ordinary mystic.

Feeding the hungry. Feeding the hungry is more than volunteering in soup kitchens or offering a handout to those in need. It is also fostering a relationship with those forgotten, marginalized, or whose situations leave them spiritually, emotionally, or psychologically hungry.

Dorothy has a younger brother who suffers from bipolar disorder. Because Bill is not always faithful to take his medication, his moods are erratic. The other family members tend to be unsympathetic to Bill's condition and hesitant to stay in touch. Dorothy, on the other hand, tries to telephone Bill daily and typically visits him twice a month. "Feeding the hungry sometimes means offering care and concern to the overlooked and forgotten," she likes to say.

Giving drink to the thirsty. Giving drink to the thirsty includes the devotion and dedication that slakes the thirst of loneliness or helps dissipate the feeling of failure. It enkindles hope in the forlorn and despondent, and fans the smoldering embers of faith in the doubtful. It glows in people who work ardently for justice and peace.

Sister Evelyn is a cloistered Poor Clare nun whose contemplative lifestyle doesn't permit her to do any kind of active ministry outside the monastery. She is deeply concerned and troubled by the increasing number of teenage suicides in our country. She prays daily for troubled teenagers. When she reads of a teenage suicide in her local newspaper, she immediately writes a note of condolence to the parents even though she doesn't know them personally.

Clothing the naked. Heidi's mission is to clothe the naked. "But I don't do it just by sharing my old clothes with the Salvation Army or the St. Vincent de Paul Society," she confesses. "I do it primarily by covering with dignity those stripped by humiliation—the children and women forced to work in sweatshops or coerced into human sex trafficking. I'm always researching companies that have manufacturing companies in Mexico and China. I post what I find on Facebook. And I help a friend raise awareness about the sex trade in Thailand." Heidi burns with a commitment to ending the use and abuse of any human being.

Sheltering the homeless. Sheltering the homeless is more than building homes with Habitat for Humanity. It is the commitment to ensure everyone has a sense of belonging and a place to call home. This love is aflame in those who work with displaced immigrants and the undocumented. It never permits one's heart to become a gated community where some are discriminated against or refused admittance. It treats everyone as a neighbor and no one as a stranger.

As a retired teacher, Jessie was moved by the plight of Syrian refugees. When she heard that a local church was fostering a family, she immediately contacted the pastor and volunteered as an English tutor. "They are going to need some basic English in order to make America their home," she told him.

Visiting the sick. "I'm just being a good neighbor," Uncle Charlie said to me, referring to his daily visits to the second floor of his nursing home. "I got to know Andrew and Lois from sitting next to them during our Sunday morning interdenominational church services in the recreation room. I like to check on them to make sure they don't have any pressing needs." Visiting this elderly couple has become Uncle Charlie's ministry, though he would be embarrassed to hear me call it that.

By visiting the sick, Bea demonstrates her care and concern for those who are infirmed, physically disabled, or unable to perform ordinary tasks because of age, injury, or infirmity. Her ministry started in the 1980s when she volunteered at Lazarus House, a home for those living with AIDS, in New Orleans. "You do for people who can't do for themselves," she says. "And you accept them right where they are." This dedication also blazes in the kindness of nurses, doctors, healthcare providers, and family caregivers.

Visiting the imprisoned. Though she is unable to visit a prison, Lisa expresses her cardiac spirituality by writing a monthly letter to an inmate on death row. Visiting the imprisoned, by post or presence, frees those shackled by any physical, emotional, or psychological chains. This loving decision tenderly illumines the jail cells found not only in detention centers and prisons, but also in the human heart—and is willing to accompany those imprisoned there.

Jack's college-age son has struggled with a drug addiction for many years. Everyone in the family has given up on Peter. Jack, however, is wise enough to know that his son has a medical problem and is stuck in a physical and psychological prison. And so, for the third time, Jack covers the costs for Peter to seek treatment at a rehabilitation center to get clean and sober. A recovering alcoholic for fifteen years, Jack knows only too well that true freedom is a process that takes time.

Burying the dead. We don't live in a culture where family members and neighbors dig their loved ones' graves. But we do live in a culture that honors the deceased with dignity, ritual, and sometimes monuments. Though death is inconvenient and disrupts our schedules and plans, we make the effort, sometimes at personal sacrifice, to attend the funerals of family and friends. Burying the dead and attending to those who are grieving are responses to the present moment.

Burying the dead also means leaving the past in the past. It radiates in spouses and friends who forgive each other and never allow an infidelity, betrayal, or angry word to be written in indelible ink. Steeped in mercy and compassion, this flame of love illumines the path to continue a journey together.

A LASTING FRUIT

When people like Cynthia mention that they are discouraged by their lack of spiritual progress, I remind them that the spiritual life is not a scorecard of spiritual experiences or a program of spiritual exercises. It's a lot more ordinary—and mystical. The spiritual life is a relationship that affects the way we live: "'You shall love the Lord your God with all your heart, and with all your soul, and with all your mind' . . . 'You shall love your neighbor as yourself.' On these two commandments hang all the law and the prophets" (Matthew 22:37, 39-40). Real spiritual progress is measured by the size of our hearts and the relentless resolve to respond to the unmet need or required duty of the present moment. At life's end, all that is left is the afterglow of our surrender, sacrifice, and service. Love and love alone is the lasting fruit of the ordinary mystic.

Practice

Revisit the seven works of mercy mentioned in this chapter. Choose one and try to practice it tomorrow either in a literal or metaphorical way.

Assess its impact on you at the end of the day.

Reflect

1. What guidelines, norms, and practices govern your own spirituality and approach to spiritual formation? How do these guidelines, norms, and practices expand the size of your heart and challenge you to love God and neighbor? How do these guidelines, norms, and practices constrict you?

2. What situations in your life give rise to the tension between a cosmetic spirituality of strictly obeying laws and a cardiac spirituality of intentional loving selflessness? How do you resolve this tension and justify your decisions and actions?

Ponder

Authentic spiritual growth is measured by Jesus' cardiac spirituality of two-fold love.

Chapter 5

INSIDES OUT

THE INVITATION TO TRANSPARENCY

I've never been good at hiding my feelings. I wear them on my sleeve, and my face instantly betrays them. Some feelings like anger, loneliness, and guilt seem to be my constant travel companions. Such feelings disrupt and sometimes hinder my prayer.

I remember once being particularly lonely. I had been on the road preaching for six consecutive weeks without a break. I felt disconnected from my community, friends, and family. I couldn't pray—every time I tried, that feeling of loneliness would well up and dampen my attempt at prayer. Rote prayer, meditative prayer, and Scripture reading all proved futile and fruitless. I decided to arrange a Skype conversation with my spiritual director to talk about my predicament.

"It sounds to me, Albert," Lucille said, "that you're trying to avoid your feeling of loneliness. Rather than trying to pray around it or in spite of it, try praying *from* your feeling of loneliness. In other words, pray from the neck down, with your heart and in your gut. Let the cat out of the bag and tell God how you feel. Spill the beans and let God know how disconnected you feel. Take what's inside and put it outside. Let your loneliness *be* your prayer as you experience it in the presence of God."

"But is that really prayer?" I asked.

"Of course! If it's an issue or problem with you, it's an issue or problem for God. And sharing it with God is a wonderful way to deepen your relationship. Prayer is about honesty and transparency."

I took her advice and tried it. I wasn't comfortable at first but gradually discovered the wisdom of befriending this emotion in my prayer. Lucille was correct. It was another way of responding to God's ardent longing and enthusiastic invitation to a deeper relationship.

FROM THE NECK DOWN

Many people pray from the neck up, making it a mental activity. They offer God praise and thanks. They talk to God about their day. They intercede for others and ask for divine favors. Others might ponder and meditate on Scripture or reflect on a belief of the Christian faith. Still others might say rote prayers or even read the prayers written by saints and holy people of the past.

Though praying in these ways has a long and hallowed tradition, it's only one side of the coin. Praying from the neck down, from a heavy heart, from the pain in your gut, with legs so weary they can't move forward, is the other side.

Jesus was comfortable with praying from the neck down. It was an aspect of his cardiac spirituality—allowing the love, mercy, humility, and compassion in his heart to rise to the surface and inform his actions. He expressed a wide range of positive and negative emotions to God and to others. The Gospel writers note, among other emotions, that he felt compassion (Matthew 15:32), was indignant (Mark 10:14), was consumed with zeal (John 2:17), was grieved (Matthew 26:38), loved (John 11:5), was greatly disturbed in spirit and deeply moved (John 11:33), and wept in sorrow (John 11:35). Matthew records him expressing surprise in a prayer of thanksgiving (Matthew 11:25-30). In Luke's Gospel, we witness his evening anguish and hear his prayer to the Father as he struggled to surrender and accept the cup of suffering (Luke 22:39-46).

> We think God is like a parent who wants to see us only on our best behavior. So we go into God's presence only when we have nothing to hide, are joy-filled, and feel we can give proper attention to God in a reverent and loving way.... We don't tell God what is really going on in our lives. We tell God what we think God wants to hear.... What's important is that we pray what's inside of us and not what we think God would like to see inside of us.... All of these feelings can be our entry into prayer. No matter the headache or the heartache, we need only to lift it up to God.
>
> Ronald Rolheiser, OMI

Jesus' example reminds us that feelings need to be experienced and emotions need to be expressed. We gladly pray from the positive feelings and emotions of joy, love, hope, gratitude, and thanksgiving. It's the negative ones such as shame, anger, loneliness, fear, nervousness, and confusion that we treat as intrusions, often trying to skirt them. If we avoid or try to suppress the negative ones, they go underground and wreak havoc on us in unhealthy, passive-aggressive ways: high blood pressure, headaches, muscle tension, ulcers, sleep disorders, binge eating or drinking, uncontrollable fits of anger, apathy, sarcasm, and inappropriate sexual actions.

To be mindful of an emotion is to acknowledge, befriend, and honor it. That is all an emotion asks of us. Once we give it that attention, it loses its power to go underground and control us. We can then strategize how best to express it in an appropriate, healthy way.

THE WELCOMING PRAYER

The Welcoming Prayer offers a practical way to be aware, acknowledge, and honor any negative emotion that makes us feel uncomfortable. It consists of three simple steps: focus and sink in, welcome, let go. The first step is to become mindful of the emotion, focus on it, and feel it as a sensation in your body. What are the physical manifestations? A tightened stomach? Sweaty palms? A frown on your face? A vengeful adrenaline surge? Tension in your shoulders? Zero in on the feeling and fully experience it. Then attempt to name it. Don't rush this step; acknowledgment of the physicality of an emotion and naming it are signs of respect for its presence and power.

After you feel and name the emotion, offer it hospitality. "Welcome, fear." "Welcome, guilt." "Welcome, anger." Be nonjudgmental toward it. Indeed, treat it as an honored guest. This is how a negative emotion is befriended. Many people find it helpful to slowly repeat the greeting for a couple of minutes as they continue to feel the emotion's sensation.

Once you have fully experienced and embraced the emotion, bid it farewell. Don't be tempted to rush this step; it's easier to suppress uncomfortable emotions—but don't. Take your time with the welcoming before you bid the feeling farewell. You might be pleasantly surprised at how an uncomfortable emotion slips away once it has been befriended and honored.

I've always had a hard time acknowledging grief. I first experienced it as a teenager with my father's death. Knowing how it engages my entire body, I've tried to suppress it or, if I can't do that, dodge it. That strategy hasn't worked very well.

A number of years ago, I noticed how easily I teared up when I saw or heard a tragic news story. I would instantly shut down my sadness. Those times indicated my discomfort with grief. I've since become quite accustomed to using the Welcoming Prayer as a way of accepting grief into my life as a normal—and healthy—human emotion.

After welcoming and honoring a negative emotion, it might choose to linger. If so, incorporate the emotion into your prayer and express it to God—or, as Lucille worded it, pray *"from* your feelings," not around them. This is a dimension of Jesus' cardiac spirituality: let what's in your heart rise to the surface and inform your prayer. Tell God how angry or hurt a friend's betrayal made you; how alone and disconnected you are from your family and friends; how frightened or nervous you are about an upcoming examination; how sad and depressed you feel at the loss of a loved one. Being mindful, befriending, and giving voice to such feelings will not only make your prayer authentic and transparent but also provide balm for a bruised or battered soul.

THE WISDOM OF EMOTIONS

Such candor and honesty can be challenging because we judge certain emotions inappropriate to bring before God. We think that feelings such as anger, shame, guilt, loneliness, fear, grief, and sexual desires have no place in the divine presence. And so, like Adam and Eve, we cover them with fig leaves.

But every emotion, no matter how unseemly we think it might be, contains a wisdom and dynamism all its own. Negative feelings are "nudgings of God." Divine treasures are often found in them if we just pause and ponder them. Their wisdom tells us something about ourselves, and their energy gives us the momentum to express that wisdom in a proper and fitting way. Just look at Jesus on the Mount of Olives: his fear was transformed into the fuel of his fortitude to face his impending death (Luke 22:39–46).

Let's consider some of the more common challenging emotions and what people have learned from being mindful of them.

Anger. Frank confided in me, "Anger makes me feel alive. I've learned it's a flashing neon arrow pointing to a wrong that needs to be righted. Its energy challenges me to stand up, speak out, and protect what I consider to be precious or important. Like a nagging teenager, it refuses to let me be. And when I pray from my anger as you taught me, Father, I open myself to the wisdom of the Spirit that informs me how to act and bring about a deeper experience of justice for myself or others." Frank has clearly learned how to befriend his anger and mine its gold.

Shame. Sheila knows shame—the feeling that overtakes a person when a morally wrong or reprehensible action is exposed—is like a burglar alarm alerting her to a breach in some necessary personal boundary. "It reminds me that sometimes I talk too much. Some personal struggles and secrets are meant to remain confidential. You're not supposed to share them nonchalantly with just anybody." As she expresses her shame to God, Sheila rediscovers how personal integrity is rooted in an appropriate privacy; this prayer prepares her for genuine intimacy with her closest friends and confidants.

Guilt. Unlike shame that typically includes exposure, guilt secretly arises when we fall short of our own moral standards. It betrays the wide divide between our ideals and our behavior. It calls us to reaffirm the commitments that give meaning and purpose to our life. When we ponder and pray over this emotion, we see how God's grace stretches us beyond the ego's obsessions with self-concern, self-image, self-gratification, and self-preservation. Guilt bids us to become ordinary mystics—and respond once again to God's invitation to a deeper relationship.

Loneliness and sexual desires. Loneliness and sexual desires have taught Matthew that he is not created to be self-sufficient and alone. They prompt him to reach out to others and strengthen his relationships in generous and virtuous ways. Praying from these feelings gives him a deeper appreciation for the healthy expression of his sexuality.

As a vowed celibate, I've spent too much time trying to suppress my sexual desires. It's an occupational hazard for many Catholic priests, nuns, and religious brothers. "They shouldn't be treated as a nuisance or the enemy," a spiritual director wisely told me. After more than forty years as a Franciscan, I've come to appreciate, befriend, and pray with these desires. Like Matthew's experience with them, sexual desires sometimes tell me I'm lonely—and so I'll visit with family and friends in person, by Skype, or by phone. But at other times they tell me I'm frustrated or under a lot of tension and stress—so I'll take a long walk or head to the gym. Mindfulness has taught me that different emotional and physical needs masquerade as sexual desires.

Fears. Michelle knows her fears are often rooted in childhood experiences. She treats those fears as friends who give advanced warning of possible danger. As she listens to them and places them in the hands of God, she is emboldened to deepen her trust. By God's grace, her fears, paradoxically, are shaping the contours of her courage.

Grief. My grief tells me that something precious is coming to an end or someone dear has died. Like fear, it challenges me to open my hands in trust to God's ardent longing and enthusiastic invitation to a deeper relationship. As I lament my loss in prayer and surrender to God's mysterious ways, the seed of hope sprouts with the promise of tomorrow and a confidence in abiding divine guidance.

Overcoming suspicion of some negative emotions is a process that takes time. We might still balk and grimace as we go to God with angry hearts, guilty consciences, or sexual desires. However, by becoming mindful of them, acknowledging them, and listening to their wisdom in the divine presence, we discover anew the encouragement they offer to continue on the pedestrian path to ordinary mysticism.

Practice

Choose an emotion that you traditionally have considered inappropriate and unseemly to bring to God in prayer. Practice the Welcoming Prayer the next time you experience it. Then begin a dialogue with God about it. Tell God how it makes you feel and why you consider it uncomfortable. Spend time listening for a response from God.

Reflect

1. Which emotions do you struggle to accept? What nuggets of wisdom can you mine from them?

2. On a scale of 1 (not at all), 2 (sometimes), 3 (often), to 4 (always), how mindful are you of your feelings? Do you recognize them instantly or does it take time to become aware of them? What techniques do you use to appropriately respond to them?

Ponder

Every feeling should be expressed to God and mined for its spiritual wisdom.

Chapter 6

A FINICKY GOD

HERE TODAY, GONE TOMORROW

*W*as it anger or confusion when Denise began a spiritual direction session by saying, "God is so finicky"?

"I beg your pardon." The comment caught me off guard.

"God is finicky. One minute he's all lovey-dovey and seducing me with such wonderful feelings that I can't help but give him my all. And then the next moment, he seems to disappear and forget he ever created me. That's when I'm tempted to say, 'Okay, be that way! You're not the only show in town. There are other fish in the pond.' And off I go—only to regret where I ended up."

Denise is an ordinary mystic. Her mindfulness and sensitivity to God's action in her life are simply amazing. When I sit with her as a spiritual director, I feel certain that God appreciates her honesty and transparency.

CONSOLATION

One recent morning while brushing my teeth and anticipating my time in prayer, I felt a strong attraction to prolonging my dedicated time with God. And I did just that—by an extra twenty-five minutes. It was a wonderful experience of almost one and a half hours that both nourished and energized my godly enthusiasm.

For the rest of the day, I felt an uncommon and continual attraction to God and other people. My gaze was focused upward as I periodically paused for a few seconds and intentionally called to mind the presence of God that surrounded me like the air I was breathing. In retrospect, I was subconsciously returning to my morning prayer time and "stretching" it into my midmorning, noon, afternoon, and evening activities. My gaze was also focused outward as I was attentive to the unmet needs of others and looked for opportunities to do simple acts of charity. Only days later did I consciously realize just how unique that day was.

> Spiritual consolation is experienced when our hearts are drawn toward God, even if this happens in circumstances that the world would regard as negative. It is a signal that our hearts, at least for that moment, are beating in harmony with the heart of God. Consolation is the experience of this deep connectedness to God, and it fills our being with a sense of peace and joy. The epicenter of the experience lies in God and not in ourselves.
>
> Margaret Silf

Ever have a day like that, when you think you are making spiritual progress? When a thought or desire draws you closer to God? When you feel on fire with spiritual enthusiasm? When you are consumed with the things of God and are eagerly responding to every moment's unmet need or required duty? The spiritual tradition refers to this experience as a consolation. More than an emotional high or a good feeling, consolations are those rare moments when God's ardent longing and enthusiastic invitation to a deeper relationship become palpable, satisfy your spiritual hunger, and leave behind a divine gift: You are uplifted, filled with interior peace and spiritual joy, and strengthened in your faith, hope, and charity. You readily yearn with an even deeper thirst to love God and neighbor that paradoxically buoys your spirit. Mindfulness of consolations is an aspect of ordinary mysticism.

How do we respond to this spiritual experience that seemingly comes out of nowhere? Knowing that we are incapable of stirring up or manufacturing it, our first response is gratitude for the inspiration and comfort it provides. Consolation is a gift that God lavishes on us with no rhyme or reason. It might last for hours or days—but never forever. Consolation is an experience of God's ardent longing. It draws us closer to God even as it encourages and emboldens our response to God's invitation.

There is always a temptation, especially for beginners in spiritual formation, to equate consolations with spiritual progress. When consolations are received, beginners mistakenly believe they are growing in the spiritual life. When consolations disappear, as they inevitably do, beginners think they are displeasing to God. However, as divine favors that are never earned, merited, or deserved, consolations do not indicate a person's spiritual maturity. As a matter of fact, a case could be made for the spiritual progress of the seasoned pilgrim who plods along, deliberately putting one foot in front of the other, without the occasional refreshment of consolations. Zach immediately comes to mind.

"Zach, how are you doing?" We were beginning our monthly spiritual direction session.

The Presbyterian minister smiled and replied, "About the same. I just keep doing what I am called to do. I spend time in devotional prayer every day. I meditate on Scripture. I work on my Sunday sermon. And I just keep trying to love, love, love the members of my congregation. That's about it."

"Has God thrown you any candy, any consolations?" I asked.

"No, not really. And that's okay. I've learned over the years that my fidelity is more important than receiving inspirational thoughts or feelings of peace and joy from God. Of course, I'll take them if God offers them. But I know it's unwise to run after them or to waste my energy trying to manufacture them."

Zach has discovered one of the great insights of the ordinary mystic: the spiritual journey is about growing in mindfulness and deepening Jesus' cardiac spirituality of two-fold love. It is not about collecting experiences and souvenirs.

DESOLATION

A person dwells in a state of desolation when she or he is moving away from God's active presence in the world. We know we are moving in this way when we sense the growth of resentment, ingratitude, selfishness, doubt, fear, and so on. If my outlook becomes increasingly gloomy and self-obsessed, I am in a state of desolation. I am resisting God or, if not actively resisting, I am being led away from God by other influences.

Vinita Hampton Wright

It's not uncommon that we experience the opposite of consolation: spiritual fatigue, discouragement, interior restlessness, sadness, disinterest, and disdain for the things of God with a keener interest in baser things. Like being in a swirling sandstorm that kicks up in the desert as we endure the noonday sun, we find our gaze focused downward and on ourselves. More than feeling bad, disappointed, or depressed, we are spiritually weary—isolated from God and others. Each step of the journey becomes heavy and hard; rather than leaning in and going forward, we want to stop or maybe even return home. The spiritual tradition refers to this experience as desolation.

Experiences of desolation typically are caused by "the spiritual forces of evil in the heavenly places" (Ephesians 6:12) whom we traditionally call Satan and the legion of devils serving him. They use experiences of desolation to sabotage and subvert our relationship with God and others. They try to convince us that our prayer, fasting, and almsgiving have been ludicrous and unhelpful in the spiritual life. They remind us of a hurt inflicted by someone and trick us into fueling a grudge—instead of responding to God's invitation to forgive. They bombard us with self-doubts and fears that cause us to second-guess the spiritual adventure and even lose interest in it. While beginners and tourists mistakenly believe they are doing something wrong and consequently are the cause of their desolation, experienced pilgrims know that this is the fickle work of Satan and, like the weather, it can change at a moment's notice.

Because the devil is conniving, experiences of desolation can be quite attractive and enticing—as someone recently reminded me, "We like to sin. Sometimes it's fun!" The devil preys on our ego obsessions and insists that happiness is having them satisfied. We sometimes give in to his seductions and temptations, later finding ourselves mired in acedia, anger, envy, greed, gluttony, lust, and pride—the seven deadly sins. As Denise said, "There are other fish in the pond. And off I go—only to regret where I ended up." Any thought or desire that leads away from God has the devil's hand in it and could potentially be an experience of desolation. That's why mindfulness is so important to the ordinary mystic.

How do we respond when desolation blankets our godly enthusiasm, and we feel we are wasting our time and energy on the spiritual journey? We remain faithful to our spiritual practices despite the superficial distaste and disinterest we currently feel for them. This is not the time to abandon or change them. Nor is this the time to make any important decisions. Fidelity to our routine of prayer and charity toward others provides a sense of continuity. Though emotionally unsatisfying, it keeps us moving forward even if we feel we've lost our way or even our road map. Such faithfulness provides its own sense of direction and sooner or later brings us to an oasis of rest.

While Brian, a spiritual directee, practices fidelity during experiences of desolation, he also reminds himself that his desolation will pass. Even though it might last for a few days and feels interminable, he knows it won't last forever. "The devil is just messin' with me," he likes to say. As a way of "returning the favor," he jokingly tells me, he thumbs his nose up at the devil and becomes intentional about extending his prayer time by ten or fifteen minutes and doing acts of charity, such as calling a homebound friend or visiting an elderly neighbor. Even though this goes against Brian's immediate desires, as an ordinary mystic, he knows spiritual intentionality goes a long way in quelling the sandstorm.

THE ABSENCE OF GOD

I spent eleven and a half years as a missionary in mainland China. One of my responsibilities was being the spiritual assistant to the Missionaries of Charity, the religious community founded by Mother Teresa of Calcutta. Periodically I would fly to Japan, South Korea,

Hong Kong, or Singapore to preach spiritual conferences and retreats to the sisters. As I gained the trust of the sisters, I began hearing rumors about their saintly founder.

> I am told God lives in me, and yet the reality of darkness and coldness and emptiness is so great that nothing touches my soul.
>
> Mother Teresa of Calcutta

With the publication of Mother Teresa's private letters to her spiritual directors in 2007, the world came to know what I had known more than a decade earlier: for almost fifty years, Mother Teresa experienced a profound spiritual darkness that felt like God had given up and abandoned her. She had no felt presence of God and no experiences of consolation. Unlike experiences of desolation that leave a distaste and disdain for the things of God, this experience plunged Mother Teresa into a vast spiritual emptiness that mimics the dark harshness and stark silence of the midnight desert. She felt spiritually cold, forgotten, and lost. Technically called the "dark night," a phrase coined by the Carmelite St. John of the Cross, her experience of the absence of God is the longest documented dark night in the history of Christian spirituality.

Many people have similar experiences when God seemingly withdraws and disappears. Steve and Stephanie were plunged into darkness as they buried their teenage daughter. Juan wondered where God was as he filed for bankruptcy. Beverly sobbed as she waited to be rescued from the roof of her flooded home, destroyed by Hurricane Harvey in August 2017. Phil was shamed and despondent over the public exposure of his past sin.

Some might argue these dark nights are not the same as for the saint from Calcutta; nevertheless, they are painfully gut-wrenching, raising doubts and questions about God's ardent longing and enthusiastic invitation to a deeper relationship.

Our initial knee-jerk reaction to the dark night is to ask, "Why would God allow this? What have I done—or not done—to deserve it?" We demand rational answers. We want to hold God accountable. But such questions assume our human intellect can understand the mysterious, incomprehensible, ineffable God, but it can't:

> For my thoughts are not your thoughts,
>   nor are your ways my ways, says the LORD.
> For as the heavens are higher than the earth,
>   so are my ways higher than your ways
> and my thoughts than your thoughts. (Isaiah 55:8-9)

Rather than searching for logical reasons for the dark night, which can lead to concocting fanciful and skewed interpretations of the mind and designs of God, the ordinary mystic searches for an appropriate response to the dark night. Two immediately come to mind.

First, as Mother Teresa's spiritual director wisely reminded her, feelings are an unsure guide in the spiritual life. Just because we *feel* that God has withdrawn and abandoned us, does not mean God, in fact, has. God's presence surrounds us like the air we breathe: "For 'In him we live and move and have our being'" (Acts 17:28). For a multitude of reasons—typically (but not always) due to an overload of certain negative feelings such as grief, guilt, shame, or regret—our senses sometimes are incapable of picking up or registering the divine presence. The five senses are not always adequate, and the feelings they stir up are not always accurate; to solely depend on either of them is to hope for refreshment in what we discover to be a mirage. Consequently, Paul reminded the Corinthians, "We walk by faith, not by sight" (2 Corinthians 5:7). In the words of the *Pange Lingua*, a hymn composed by St. Thomas Aquinas, "Faith for all defects supplying, / Where the feeble senses fail." At times, all we can muster is an emotionally flat, intellectual assent to what we struggle to believe: God is always present—even in the midst of darkness.

Second, besides calling us to disregard and distrust our feelings, the dark night challenges us to let go of our beloved, trusted, and time-tested images of God. Indeed, the dark night strips them from us. References to God as an eternal Father of unconditional love or a divine Mother of infinite compassion wither and crumble in the frigid, arid, and silent darkness of this night. Think of Jesus, struggling on the cross to make sense of his image of God as Abba as he begins to pray Psalm 22, "My God, my God, why have you forsaken me?" (Matthew 27:46). This purification reminds us that our God images are as different from the reality of God as a photograph is from its subject. We give up the false security of thinking we know God and abandon ourselves in faith and trust to the divine personal mystery of unconditional love at the heart of our existence. "Thy will be done." This surrender of the heart becomes the dark night's North Star pointing to the horizon of mysticism.

Mindfulness of where thoughts, desires, and feelings are leading—to God or away from God—is a helpful practice. While God uses consolations to attract and nourish us, Satan uses desolations to discourage and misguide us. And sometimes, as experienced pilgrims know, feelings cannot be trusted. Ordinary mystics are always watching for the myriad ways God invites them to a deeper relationship.

Practice

Sit comfortably and quietly in a chair. Take a few deep breaths and come back to the present moment. Once you have arrived, become aware of your thoughts, desires, and feelings at this very moment. Spend twenty minutes being mindful of them and watching them.

After the twenty minutes have passed, ask yourself: *Are my thoughts, desires, and feelings pointing me to a deeper relationship with God or away from God?*

Having answered the question, decide on a specific action as an appropriate response.

Reflect

1. Recall a recent time when you experienced consolation. How did it energize or encourage you? How did you respond to it? Recall a recent time when you experienced desolation. How did it affect you? How did you respond to it?

2. How have you experienced the dark night? What advice would you give a trusted friend who is going through it?

Ponder

God's presence surrounds us like the air we breathe.

Chapter 7

GROPING IN THE DARK

WALKING BY FAITH, NOT SIGHT

*A*fter more than ten years as a missionary in mainland China, my cover was blown, and the Chinese government found out who I was, where I lived, and what I was doing. Against my will but knowing it was a wise decision, I returned to the United States in January 2004. I thought I was coming home, but I quickly discovered I was a stranger in a foreign land. Listening to the radio and watching television brought back memories of my first days in China when I couldn't understand what I was hearing or relate to what I was watching. There were at least three generations of Franciscans who knew me only as "the friar in China." My Franciscan classmates were still relating to me as they had done a decade earlier; they were unaware that China had changed me. My best friends, all Chinese, were now on the other side of the world; despite Skype and email, I knew our friendships would never be the same. Even the food tasted strange to me, as I yearned for home style tofu, Beijing noodles, and hot pot. I felt as if I had been plopped in the middle of a mid-night desert with no night-vision goggles, map, or survival kit.

I had decided with my religious superior to fill the need for a theology professor at our small university in southern Illinois. I taught at Quincy University for two years and was miserable. Though I enjoyed relative success in the classroom and was sought after as a confidant and mentor by some of my students, I was a lost soul. Because my self-image had been so tied up with being a missionary to China, I struggled to find meaning as a university professor. I was deflated, discouraged, and depressed.

Why had God allowed the Chinese government to discover my true identity and thus bring an end to my forty-five-year-old dream of being a missionary to China? What now was my calling and vocation? How could I repair a life that was not only unraveling at the edges but also torn in two?

TIMES OF QUESTIONS AND CONFUSION

Unlike a dark night that suddenly descends and stifles with the absence of God, there are other times of profound confusion, questioning, and anxiety. We turn in on ourselves and become self-absorbed. We are pushed down steps into a dark, sweltering basement where we stumble and struggle to find a ray of light. We gasp for meaning as the fumes of our faith dissipate and an emotional upheaval, clouding our vision, kicks up doubts about the future. We feel disoriented, lost, and forgotten as a deafening silence reigns in our lives. Like the Israelites in the desert grumbling against Moses, we ask, "Why did you bring us out of Egypt, to kill us and our children and livestock with thirst?" (Exodus 17:3). I call such times moments of mystery. We all have experienced them.

Philip and Ann are committed to their faith and bring their Christian values to their work. They awaited the birth of their third child with joyful anticipation. But little Julie lived for fewer than seventy-two hours. "Why did God let us get so excited only to disappoint us?" they asked as they were plunged into a moment of mystery.

Many people thought Sally was being naive. But when her husband, after his two years of infidelity, begged to start their marriage all over again, Sally nodded with confused hesitancy. The ambiguity of her willingness was a step into darkness.

> Nothing new happens as long as we are inside our self-constructed comfort zone. Nothing good or creative emerges from business as usual. Much of the work of the God of the Bible is to get people into liminal space ("a narrow place without answers"), and to keep them there long enough so they can learn something essential. It is the ultimate teachable space, maybe the only one.
>
> Richard Rohr

The phone call from the adoption agency proved to be a test of Sue and Andy's generosity and faith. The little boy had been found in a plastic bag in a garbage dumpster. He was a few months old and severely brain damaged. "We know you and Sue have been interested in a child. This one will be virtually impossible to place. You are our only hope. Will you accept him?" Andy could not walk away from such a child. Though he understood Sue's initial opposition, he was not at peace. He wrestled for a week with a decision. Convincing Sue, he returned the adoption agency's call. "Yes, we'll give the little boy a home." Andy and Sue said yes to a moment of mystery that raised more questions than answers.

A friend of mine in his early forties announced to his wife one day, "I need some space. I need some time to be alone. I need some freedom." That precipitated a moment of mystery for my friend's wife of fifteen years; she had to live with confusing, heart-breaking questions that weren't immediately answered: "What's wrong? Will he return? What did I do?"

RESPONDING TO MYSTERY

How do we respond to such times of disorientation when we either feel paralyzed to move or find ourselves wandering aimlessly with no sense of direction? What do we do when our self-image is stripped away from us? How do we deal with the surprise of unexpected and sudden change? What do we do when we are discontent with the present, the future has yet to reveal itself, and we feel like we are hanging in midair? How do we live with the haunting question, "Why me?" Mindfulness of the present moment can be an agony when the moment seems like a confusing or empty, meaningless void.

Some people make the mistake I made after returning to the United States. Rather than living in the present and allowing the future to unfold in its own way and time, I clung to my past self-image as a missionary and stubbornly kept one foot in China. I spent endless hours having Skype conversations and emailing my Chinese friends. I ate in Chinese restaurants, visited Chinese websites, and listened to Chinese radio stations. I was my own worst enemy, because denial is the fuel of frustration.

> Some people will never learn anything because they grasp too soon. Wisdom, after all, is not a station you arrive at, but a manner of traveling. . . . To know exactly where you're headed may be the best way to go astray. Not all who loiter are lost.
>
> Anthony de Mello

Some people search for mystery's meaning using the time-tested device of logic's light. They foolishly use the mind to deconstruct mystery with pat answers and illumine it with rational understanding. They pick away at mystery, hoping to crack its secret and analyze it like a specimen under a microscope. "This will make me a better person." "God is trying to teach me a lesson." "This is God's way of disciplining me." But Scripture reveals that logic cannot illumine what can only be found beyond its light, in the darkness of faith. That's why John of the Cross wisely reminds us that "[humans] must keep their eyes shut and tread the path in darkness if they want to be sure of where they are going."

Job is a biblical example of someone who tread the path of mystery in darkness. This upright, God-fearing man suddenly had everything taken away from him: family, farm, health (see Job 1:6-19). Questions swirl like a sandstorm as the ego's obsessions with self-concern, self-image, self-gratification, and self-preservation are confronted and contested. Still trusting in God (Job 1:21-22), Job surrendered in silence for seven days and seven nights (Job 2:13).

Job's friends, Eliphaz, Bildad, and Zophar, were convinced they knew why righteous Job was suffering. In lengthy speeches spanning twenty-two chapters (Job 4-25), they tell Job that his suffering was a result of a sin. If he admitted it and repented, God would bless him again. Though Job later admits he overstated his righteousness (Job 42:1-6), God flatly refused his friends' interpretation as "folly" (Job 42:8).

And then there is Joseph, steeped in his confusion. His fiancée is pregnant and he is not the father of the child. His uncertainty and skepticism caused him to consider breaking his engagement with Mary. An angel appears to him and tells him that Mary is pregnant by the Holy Spirit. Joseph is asked to take the pregnant woman into his home, to care for her, and to name the child Jesus (Matthew 1:18-25). A moment of mystery. A call to walk in the darkness.

Joseph would have been beating his head against a brick wall if he had tried to make sense of the Annunciation. And those rational people who criticized him for taking a pregnant woman into his home and marrying her? They betray their own ignorance of the ways of God. Richard Rohr writes, "People who have really met the Holy are always humble. It's the people who don't know who usually pretend that they do. People who've had any genuine spiritual experience always know they don't know. They are utterly humbled before mystery. They are in awe before the abyss of it all."

> Father,
> I abandon myself into your hands.
> Do with me what you will.
> Whatever you may do, I thank you.
> I am ready for all; I accept all.
> Let only your will be done in me
> and in all your creatures.
> I wish no more than this, O Lord.
> Into your hands I commend my soul.
> I offer it to you with all the love of my heart,
> for I love you, Lord, and so need to give myself,
> to surrender myself into your hands
> without reserve and with boundless confidence,
> for you are my Father.
>
> *Charles de Foucauld*

Mystery demands at least passive resignation, at most, abandonment and trustful surrender. There is no other response. The challenge of the midlife transition can only be endured, not explained. The birth of a sick child defies both faith and logic. Compelling interior stirrings can't always be rationalized or explained. How often have we heard ourselves say, "I don't know why, but I just have to trust my gut on this one"? Moments of mystery call us to become mystics of darkness as we walk with all of our doubts and uncertainties beyond the light, into an apparent abyss. We slowly and hesitantly feel our way through faith's darkness not knowing if we are moving backward, forward, or retracing our steps. To walk in this darkness is to journey through mystery's birth canal.

While on a preaching mission in Cameroon, West Africa, I met a man named John who had been born blind. We talked daily during those three weeks, and I once asked him if he found it difficult not having eyesight. He surprised me with his response, "Don't you know? Haven't you experienced it? After all, when it comes to living our faith, we all walk as blind people."

To befriend and walk with mystery is to embrace the blindness of faith. Faith is a verb, not a noun; it is a way of living, not simply believing. It is our response to God's invitation to a deeper relationship. We let go of the past's familiarity and comfort. We also renounce the ego's need to understand and rationalize that offers so much false security and, like Peter, take that agonizing and precarious step onto water (Matthew 14:29). What is important is not how far we get; the important thing is that we take the step. Ordinary mystics know well that faith and spiritual maturity are measured in the stepping, not in the size of the stride.

"BABY STEPS"

Father Medard grew old graciously. Ironically, some forty of his eighty-eight years presented physical and psychological challenges. A bout with tuberculosis, an operation removing half his lung, and fifteen other operations, including one on his heart, left him with a frail physical presence. Surprisingly, though, he had more ministerial energy than friars half his age.

Medard was never elected to any position among the friars. One could say he had been ostracized by his own Franciscan community. He was the rector of the Franciscan theology school during the tumultuous years of change immediately after Vatican II. The older priests and the faculty of the theology school thought Medard was too progressive. The students complained he was too conservative. Stuck in the middle and totally misunderstood, he had no friends or confidants among the friars.

Such physical trials coupled with his community's lack of appreciation and understanding would have turned many people bitter, angry, and resentful. But that didn't happen to Medard. He had no guile or axes to grind.

As I teared up before his open coffin in July 2004 and gazed upon his corpse wearing his bulky, orthopedic shoes, I remembered a conversation we had had that revealed the secret to his mysticism. "Baby steps, Albert," he confided to me, "baby steps. You just respond to God's grace by putting one foot in front of the other, even if it's just a hesitant shuffle."

As we shuffle in the darkness of faith, as we take baby steps with the doubts of midlife down a path we never have been before, as we stand before the mystery of a sick child or the loss of a beloved person, the mystery, like a cactus flower, slowly buds, breaks open, and begins to blossom—and we find our resignation or surrender transformed into willing acceptance as we pray the ordinary mystic's prayer, "Thy will be done." At this moment, the dawn of a new day with its glimmer of light appears on the horizon as mystery gives birth to meaning. How many times have we heard ourselves say, "I never would have thought that something this good could have come out of something that started so badly"? Or, "If you would

have told me back then what I know now, I would not have been
so frightened and resistant."

Job's innocent suffering gave birth to insights into the sovereign
plan of the ineffable Creator. In the end, God blessed Job with twice
as much as he had before (Job 42:10). For Joseph, the mystery of
the Annunciation blossomed into the miracle of Christmas. For those
in the midlife transition, the devastating questions and restlessness,
which challenge and threaten the ego obsessions of the first half of
life, gradually become silent; these people then begin the interior
spiritual journey that is the usual task of the second half of life. The
lonely and frightening walk to embrace one's own sexuality brings
a person one step closer to self-acceptance and personal integration.
Even the profound mystery of a stillborn child flowers into the
realization of a life's mission quietly and quickly completed.

My attempts to hang on to my self-image as a missionary and
keep one foot in China continued for two years. I wrestled with the
questions, "Why did I return to the States? What am I doing here?
What is God asking of me?" I lived with constant frustration. As
the months passed, the emails to Chinese friends gradually became
less frequent. I found myself eating more often in Burger King than
in the Emperor's Palace. I accepted occasional speaking invitations.
Those invitations became more frequent—so much so that I received
permission to become a full-time itinerant preacher.

One evening in Laramie, Wyoming, I preached about life's disap-
pointments and sorrows. As an example, I shared how my childhood
dream of being a missionary to China came to a sudden halt. I spoke
about my continued regret, even after four years, of no longer being
a missionary.

After the service, a woman approached me and thanked me for
my words. She continued, "Father, after hearing your story, I couldn't

help but think, with all the traveling and preaching that you do, you're still very much a missionary—but not in a foreign land. You're a missionary to your own country!"

I was taken aback by those words. I had never thought of myself as a missionary to the United States. With that sudden new perspective, a morning's light dawned upon me. I was born again as mystery blossomed into meaning.

Thomas Merton's famous prayer is one to pray during a moment of mystery. This could have been Job's or Joseph's prayer. It certainly was mine. When we are called to befriend mystery, to live with a question, to grope in the darkness, we pray:

> My Lord God, I have no idea where I am going. I do not see the road ahead of me. I cannot know for certain where it will end. Nor do I really know myself, and the fact that I think I am following your will does not mean that I am actually doing so. But I believe that the desire to please you does in fact please you. And I hope I have that desire in all that I am doing. I hope that I will never do anything apart from that desire. And I know that if I do this you will lead me by the right road, though I may know nothing about it. Therefore I will trust you always though I may seem to be lost and in the shadow of death. I will not fear, for you are ever with me, and you will never leave me to face my perils alone.

Practice

Spend time journaling the completion to the following sentences:

- The most challenging time in my life was . . .
- In my confusion, I questioned God when . . .
- A moment of mystery that later gave birth to new meaning and a new perspective for me was . . .

Consider sharing the responses with a spiritual companion or trusted friend.

Reflect

1. When have you felt like Job and suffered innocently? When have you felt like Joseph and been challenged to walk in faith? How have the stories of Job and Joseph touched you, impressed you, or challenged you?

2. Prayerfully reflect on the words of Thomas Merton's prayer. What memories does it awaken in you?

Ponder

To walk in the darkness of mystery is to be led by the light of faith.

Chapter 8

CHALLENGING THE EGO

FORGIVING GOD, MYSELF, AND OTHERS

*J*t took me fifteen years to come to grips with the reality of my
father's suicide. In my late twenties as I was preparing for ordination to the priesthood, I decided to seek out short-term counseling
to tie up any emotional loose ends remaining from my childhood.
What I thought was going to be at most a twelve-week detour into
the past turned into a fifteen-month odyssey.

In the fourth session with my counselor, I had a disconcerting
surprise about myself that I couldn't deny. I had always thought of
myself as a fun-loving, jolly person—and I was. But underneath that
veneer of joy was someone filled with anger.

I was angry at my father for the decision he had made. I thought
him selfish and self-centered for doing something that had severe
ramifications for the entire family. Wasn't he aware of the hurt his
decision would cause the family and the financial burdens he would
place on the shoulders of my mother, who had been a stay-at-home

mom? Had he forgotten his responsibility as a parent to his two daughters and three sons?

I played and replayed memories of when I had disrespected my father just a week before his death. I was certain my teenage antics of acting out disappointed him and played a role in his decision to die by suicide. I bitterly regretted my actions and was angry at myself.

I was also angry with God for allowing this to happen. If God was all-knowing, all-powerful, and unconditionally loving, why hadn't he made the gun malfunction or deflected the bullet from entering my father's chest? Why hadn't God challenged my conscience days before and reminded me to honor my father? Where was God on that Tuesday afternoon in October 1968?

The present moment is an ambassador that declares the will of God in the unmet need or required duty. Sometimes it's a challenge to respond to the required duty. I spent many months of counseling circling in a desert of anger, bitterness, and regret as I struggled to accept God's invitation to forgive.

THE ROAD MAP TO FORGIVENESS

My father's death was my first experience with resentment born of anger. It helped form my preoccupation with self-preservation: Because my mother had only a high school education and spent her adult life as a stay-at-home mother, how would we survive? How would food get on the table, and how could we afford a roof over our heads? It also formed my preoccupation with self-image: suicide in the 1960s was stigmatized, something whispered about among only the closest of friends. For some irrational reason, it made me and my family feel guilty and responsible. At age thirteen, I was too young to know what I discovered in my later twenties: forgiving my father would partly entail moving beyond a preoccupation with self-preservation and self-image; it would also require reframing my thoughts about the true meaning of happiness.

Many people don't think of forgiveness as a spiritual practice. But it is. And it's one of the most challenging. It requires moving beyond the hurts that emerge when people malign our reputations, don't live up to our expectations, or gossip behind our backs. It requires refusing to fiddle with the resentments that bubble up when friends and acquaintances criticize our lifestyles or hurt us. It requires not picking at the grudges that fester when companions and family denigrate and disparage what we hold near and dear. Forgiveness threatens and confronts any fixation with self-concern, self-image, self-gratification, and self-preservation. It calls for freedom from the ego's stranglehold.

Freedom from the ego—gained through mindfulness, changing our thoughts by thinking with the Sermon on the Mount, and responding to God's ardent longing and enthusiastic invitation to a deeper relationship—is a lifelong, slow process consisting more of uneven, faltering baby steps than long, celebratory strides. But every step away from the ego gets us closer to authentic, enduring forgiveness. As we grow in mindfulness of our thoughts and desires right here, right now, and stop feeding the four obsessions, the ego begins to deflate, and we no longer have the need to harbor animosity. We let go of the past and come back to living in the present moment. Because it's easy to slip, fall, and revert back to past anger, grudges, and resentments, Jesus' advice in the Sermon on the Mount is well taken: "But I say to you, love your enemies and pray for those who persecute you" (Matthew 5:44). Praying for my deceased father, even before I came to forgive him, kept me on the long road toward the oasis of forgiveness.

I disagreed with a friend who said, "To forgive my wife is like giving her permission to slap me in the face again." Forgiveness does not mean we approve or condone the sin, transgression, or offense committed against us. It does not mean we renounce healthy self-esteem and become a doormat where others wipe their feet. It faces the truth, acknowledges the debt owed, and names the wrong for what it is (see the parable of the unforgiving servant, Matthew 18:23-35). But it does ignore the ego by replacing its demand for justice with a donation of mercy and compassion—that's a way to live the cardiac spirituality of Jesus.

Though I knew I could never change the fact of my father's death, I mistakenly thought the path to forgiveness lay in erasing its memory. When an important event like my college graduation or my ordination to the priesthood made my father's absence conspicuous again, I was advised, "Forget it, don't dwell on it, and move on with your life!" Try as I did, unfortunately, I could not follow that advice—to suppress his memory.

Forgiving does not mean forgetting. When we forgive a person, the memory of the wound might stay with us for a long time, even throughout our lives. Sometimes we carry the memory in our bodies as a visible sign. But forgiveness changes the way we remember. It converts the curse into a blessing. When we forgive our parents for their divorce, our children for their lack of attention, our friends for their unfaithfulness in crisis, our doctors for their ill advice, we no longer have to experience ourselves as the victims of events we had no control over.

Forgiveness allows us to claim our own power and not let these events destroy us; it enables them to become events that deepen the wisdom of our hearts. Forgiveness indeed heals memories.

Henri J. Nouwen

"Forgive and forget" is advice often given but sometimes impossible to heed. Indeed, some hurts—the death of a loved one by suicide or murder, adultery, financial fraud, or personal deception—are seared on our memory. "How can I forget the way he blatantly lied to me?" Michelle asked. "I'd be lying to myself if I said I could."

To forgive is not to forget: I remember but choose not to go down the ego's rabbit hole with its labyrinthine maze of maniacal protests and narcissistic complaints. Forgiveness is memory enshrined in mercy.

Anger, resentment, and grudges are heavy loads to carry under the desert sun. They drain us of much-needed energy as we struggle to keep them balanced on our backs. We grow weary. We often forget that the people who wronged us have gone on with their journeys—and are enjoying life! Forgiveness is a gift we give, not to the betrayer, but to *ourselves*, that unburdens and refreshes our spirits.

Forgiveness is not a feeling but a decision. It begins with an act of the will that ever so gradually deflates the ego and influences the heart. Like any other commitment or resolution, it is not an action that has an instantaneous effect on our mindset and perspective. It is more like a process: we remind ourselves of our decision and renew our resolve whenever the ego bangs its fist on the table and demands revenge.

Those fifteen months of therapy taught me both the nature of forgiveness and some techniques to practice when the present moment's required duty is to forgive God, myself, or others.

FORGIVING GOD

"It sounds to me like you need to forgive God," the priest said to me.

"Forgive *God*?" I asked. "I wouldn't have the nerve to be angry with God. That's not even in the realm of possibility. That would be a serious sin."

Forgiving God sounds blasphemous. It implies that God commits sin, practices injustice, and even has done wrong. Jesus stressed the exact opposite: God is "generous" (Matthew 20:15) and unconditionally loving, making "his sun rise on the evil and on the good, and send[ing] rain on the righteous and on the unrighteous" (Matthew 5:45). Evil intent and partiality are antithetical to the God revealed in Jesus.

And yet, without being consciously aware of our feelings, some of us blame God and even hold grudges against God. I did for almost fifteen years. We pray for good, honorable, and even admirable things—for the unemployed, world peace, the end of terrorism—and our prayers go unanswered. We read about natural disasters like hurricanes, tornadoes, and tsunamis that destroy lives and livelihoods and wonder why God doesn't stop them. Why does God make some children suffer terrible, life-threatening diseases or, even worse, make some parents bury their children? The catalog of complaints is endless. Perhaps you know a friend or relative who, walking away from God and any association with a church, has pointed a finger of blame and shame at the heavens because of some disappointment, suffering, or tragedy.

Forgiving God involves maintaining a childlike relationship and personal investment with the divine when the ego becomes resentful, cynical, or skeptical. The heart of the Judeo-Christian revelation reminds us that God is a personal, loving, and compassionate mystery. As a *personal* mystery, God is ardently invested in our individual lives and longs for us to experience life in abundance (see John 10:10). God *loves* us unconditionally, even with our sin (see Romans 5:8). As a *compassionate* mystery, God is moved by our suffering and struggles (see Exodus 3:7). But, above all, God is an ineffable, incomprehensible *mystery* (see Isaiah 55:8-9).

Maintaining a relationship with the divine amid our unanswered prayers and sufferings requires the childlike attitude that believes

God, like any other parent or guardian, can be trusted and knows our predicament—even when we do not understand the deafening silence or agree with the apparent response. That childlike trust begins to bud in adults who accept the present moment and pray the prayer of Jesus in the garden of Gethsemane, "Not my will but yours be done" (Luke 22:42); it blossoms in a final act of abandonment and surrender: "Father, into your hands I commend my spirit" (Luke 23:46). Forgiving God is a radical—perhaps *the* most radical—act of faith and fidelity that forges a footpath to freedom from the ego. This is the stance of an ordinary mystic.

There's a simple prayer technique that can help you maintain this radical faith during difficult times when you might be tempted toward anger and resentment toward God.

Begin by adopting a sitting position that is comfortable and keeps you attentive. As you settle into this position, call to mind that you are in the presence of God, who is a personal, loving, and compassionate mystery. Spend ample time basking in the awareness of this all-encompassing presence right here, right now.

Bring your present situation to this presence. As you do so, make a conscious effort not to analyze your difficulty, find meaning in your suffering, or answer the nagging question, "Why me?" As a child of God, assume you will not understand God's loving, compassionate designs and mysterious manner of working in the world. This step is walking with a moment of mystery and dismantles the ego's attempt to fix, control, or understand every incident and circumstance.

As you sit in the presence of God before your situation, slowly inhale as you pray the word *acceptance*. This imitates the prayer of Jesus in the garden of Gethsemane. As you exhale, pray the word *surrender*. This imitates the prayer of Jesus from the cross.

The more we practice it, the more this technique challenges the ego and strengthens our resolve to accept the invitation to forgive God.

FORGIVING MYSELF

We live in a perfection-driven world with unrealistic expectations that other people put on us or that we put on ourselves. Consequently, we make mistakes by omission and commission that we bitterly regret. We fail at some major life project: our marriage ends in divorce or a company we start goes bankrupt. Some people feel guilty because they hurt someone they love: Betty betrayed her spouse; Raymond was forced to put his ailing father in a nursing home. Others beat themselves up because of the harm caused by self-destructive behaviors: one's smoking leads to cancer, or one's addiction destroys a family. We regret not doing something we thought we should have done: we didn't intervene in a family dispute, weren't present at the death of a loved one, or didn't put enough money away for an adequate retirement. It's so easy to become lost in a desert of regrets, sorrows, and sins.

> If the Catholicism that I was raised in had a fault, and it did, it was precisely that it did not allow for mistakes. It demanded that you get it right the first time. . . .
> We need a theology of brokenness . . .
> We need a theology that tells us that mistakes are not forever, that they are not even for a life-time, that time and grace wash clean, that nothing is irrevocable. Finally, we need a theology which teaches us that God loves us as sinners and that the task of Christianity is not to teach us how to live, but how to live again, and again, and again.
>
> Ronald Rolheiser, OMI

Finding the way to a clear conscience where one is revived and refreshed by self-forgiveness requires practicing CPR. The C stands for *confession*. Forgiving oneself begins with admitting the mistake or fault to a trusted friend, a family member, or a member of the clergy. An undisclosed regret becomes like a woodpecker chiseling at our conscience; it can easily turn into a festering wound. "You're only as sick as your secrets," to quote a saying of twelve-step programs. Once acknowledged, a fault or sin loses its hidden power over us. Confession silences the nagging guilt pecking at our inner peace.

Even after we have admitted our mistake, it's always tempting to return to the scene of the crime and relive the memory. But a diet of regurgitated memories is unhelpful and unhealthy. The second step of CPR is *pressing* the stop button: leave the past in the past. If you insist on dwelling on the past, think about all the good things you have done in your life. On occasion, we all have lived Jesus' cardiac spirituality and valiantly surrendered, sacrificed, and served others to our own surprise! Focus on those memories. They often bespeak and betray our truest character.

The R stands for *relaxation*. It's so easy to be more demanding than God and burden ourselves with thoughts of perfection.

"Cut yourself some slack. If God wanted you to be perfect, he would have made you a computer without free will," a priest once advised me. He continued, "We all have things in our past that we bitterly regret. But rather than unjustly judging a past action based on today's wisdom and maturity, celebrate how God's grace has touched and transformed you since the incident."

This third step is not a denial of the past or a refusal to accept responsibility for an action. Rather, it is a realistic acknowledgment of human frailty, our growth in maturity, and, above all, the transformative power of God's grace.

A regular practice of CPR promotes a healthy understanding of how God's ardent longing and enthusiastic invitation to a deeper relationship interact and transform pilgrims into ordinary mystics.

FORGIVING OTHERS

Forgiving another person is another direct affront to the ego. As I have already mentioned, it is a process that begins with an act of the will, a decision, a resolve. Praying for the betrayer or enemy helps to facilitate that decision and keeps the process moving along.

However, the ego tries to sabotage each and every movement toward mercy by putting up a firewall of anger. Behind that firewall are unresolved—and sometimes unspoken—feelings that hinder one's journey toward forgiveness. Unexpressed expectations take cover under darkness and betray the fact that we hold people accountable for what we don't tell them. Repressed grievances sometimes are buried in the sands of childhood. Unfulfilled hopes and their resulting resentments are symptomatic of the way we live *around* our wounds.

> The parable is not just about the Prodigal Son. It is about two prodigal sons. The elder brother turns out to be a bigger sinner than the younger. He is the chief prodigal because he refuses to forgive.
>
> *Thomas Keating*

The parable of the prodigal son clearly highlights unexpressed feelings behind the firewall of anger. The elder son was unwilling to celebrate his younger brother's return home because of an unresolved childhood complaint against his father's perceived injustice: "Listen! For all these years I have been working like a slave for you, and I have never disobeyed your command; yet you have never given me even a young goat so that I might celebrate with my friends. But when this son of yours came back, who has devoured your property with prostitutes, you kill the fatted calf for him!" (Luke 15:29-30). His anger and resentment uncovered a deeper wound: frustrated in his attempts to satisfy his ego's obsession to win his father's approval, attention, and affection, the elder son felt taken for granted and ignored.

Divorced for twelve years, Carolyn still was angry and bitter. "I just can't believe Conrad could say, 'I do,' and then fifteen months later, say he wants a divorce. He made me look like a fool. Everyone keeps asking me, 'What did you do?' I tell them I didn't do anything, and yet I just know they don't believe me. I don't think I ever will be able to trust another man again."

"I certainly understand your feeling of betrayal," I replied. "But do you have any idea *why* he wanted a divorce?"

"To be truthful with you," Carolyn said, "I saw it coming early on. Conrad was immature in a lot of ways. And I think he didn't know what a commitment in marriage was all about."

I noted Carolyn's mindfulness and her hesitation to respond to the situation.

We continued to discuss her anger and sense of betrayal as well as Conrad's immaturity for two spiritual direction sessions. Ever so gradually, Carolyn came to see her marriage from Conrad's perspective. That helped her not only to understand his immaturity, but also to let go of her anger and bitterness.

Climbing over the firewall of anger and placing one's feet in the shoes of the betrayer, to understand the betrayer's heart, can help foster forgiveness. That's what Carolyn did. What external factors could have influenced the person? What emotional wound could have prompted the person to respond to us in such a way? What possible pain could have motivated the betrayer? Pondering these questions sometimes will give rise to an insight of understanding. Empathy paves a path to forgiveness as we recognize and accept the brokenness of every human heart.

This was the strategy of the prodigal son's father as he pleaded with his elder son to accept a parent's unconditional love and understand the capricious behavior of a youth. "Son, you are always with me, and all that is mine is yours. But we had to celebrate and rejoice, because this brother of yours was dead and has come to life; he was lost and has been found" (Luke 15:31-32). Stepping into the shoes of the younger son with compassion certainly did not absolve or exonerate the younger son from breaking his father's trust. It simply acknowledged the younger son as being as fragile as anyone else.

I found the oasis of forgiveness when I came to understand my father's alcoholism and discovered news about a secret financial debt he had amassed. These revelations made me realize his choice to die by his own hand was influenced by factors that clearly impaired his judgment. Something snapped inside of him on October 22, 1968, and he could not see himself continuing to live for another day. My decision to forgive was a way to honor a life laden with burdens, struggles, and secrets.

Ordinary mystics accept—sometimes easily, sometimes with a struggle—this moment's invitation to forgive God, themselves, or others. As they do, they discover a path leading to a refuge from the unrelenting taskmaster of the ego. In the shade of that refuge, they discover a new depth of faith in God, a surer acceptance of themselves, and a selfless hospitality to welcome those once considered the enemy.

Practice

Think back to a recent tragedy, disappointment, or unanswered prayer. Practice for fifteen minutes the breathing technique of forgiving God.

Upon completion, ask yourself: *How challenging was it? How helpful was it in leading me to surrender, sacrifice, and service?*

Reflect

1. For what do you still have to forgive yourself? How would each step of CPR help facilitate the decision and process?

2. Think of someone you still need to forgive. How can you develop understanding and empathy for the person?

Ponder

The process of forgiveness is another practical way to be set free from the obsessions of the ego.

Chapter 9

INSPIRED BY JESUS

REDISCOVERING GOD

I am becoming more and more uncomfortable with Pope Francis. I just don't understand why he's doing what he's doing," Charlotte said. "I really think he's betraying God."

"Betraying *God*? What do you mean?" I asked.

"God expects us to obey both his Word and the way the church always has interpreted it. But Pope Francis is showing no respect for either of them. He's promoting acceptance of gays. He wants priests to 'accompany' people who are divorced and remarried. I'm not sure what he means by that, but it sounds like he is changing church law. He's putting so much emphasis on love, mercy, and compassion that he's watering down our faith. God expects us to stand up for the truth and have backbone; that's why he gave us the Ten Commandments. We just can't change our beliefs because society or the government says something is okay."

"Is the pope really changing our beliefs, or is he helping us rediscover some of their fundamental principles? After all, didn't Jesus command us to be loving, merciful, and compassionate? Remember he said that we must be perfect as God is perfect," I gently responded.

Charlotte looked at me with challenging eyes. "God demands *obedience* first." She emphasized the word by using her index finger and underlining it with an imaginary horizontal line in the air. "And then come love, mercy, and compassion. He's very clear on this."

I paused and decided to change the topic of conversation when I saw Charlotte's tense facial expression. Only later, upon reflection, did I discover what was behind Charlotte's intensity: her displeasure with Pope Francis had more to do with a perceived threat to her image of God than with the pontiff's vision of Catholicism.

Isn't that the case for many of the religious beliefs and doctrines we hold tightly? Because we live on autopilot, we are not mindful of how they are inextricably bound to our image of God. When someone questions one of those beliefs, we unconsciously think that person is threatening and casting doubt on our image of God. As a result, we become defensive and sometimes confrontational.

A COMPASS FOR THE JOURNEY

Your image of God is one of the most important aspects of your spirituality and, like a compass, points you in a specific direction. The reasons why you pray, obey the commandments, fast, accept suffering, give alms, attend church services, confess sin, hold on to hope, and practice the virtues are rooted in how you think about God.

God might be for you a divine parent, lover, or friend who watches over you and with whom you want to spend time in prayer; a policeman who monitors your actions and is quick to catch any violation of the law; a heavenly Santa Claus who needs to be informed and coaxed; a creator who dazzles you daily with daffodils and daisies; the distant "man upstairs" who has to be appeased with praise and worship; an avenger who has the need to balance the scales of justice with a tit-for-tat; a wisdom figure reminiscent of an elderly grandparent; an abiding presence that surrounds you like the air you breathe; the master puppeteer pulling the strings of life; a stern teacher of morality who commands obedience; a judge sitting on the bench of the court of last resort. How you think about God determines the direction your spiritual journey takes.

Charlotte's God seems to be a stern teacher who commands obedience. This not only influenced her displeasure with Pope Francis but also colored how she herself related to God. Did she actively choose such an image of God? Probably not. Just like yours, her compass was determined by personal, religious, and cultural factors.

Parents or guardians often imprint on us the first image of God. I vividly remember being four or five years old and my mother

One day, Angelica spread out all her crayons and bent over a large piece of paper. For a long time, she worked and concentrated as hard as she could. When her older brother came by and asked what she was doing, she replied, "I'm drawing a picture of God." The brother smirked and said, "Nobody knows what God looks like!" Angelica simply replied, "They will when I'm finished!"

While we may have never tried to draw God's picture, we all have implicit images of God, some of which we have articulated, some of which are all the more powerful for not having been brought to consciousness. Our hymns, religious art and the prayers we've learned have all subtly shaped our theology from the time we could focus or understand the words we heard.

Mary M. McGlone

bringing me to church "to visit with Jesus." As she knelt in prayer and I fidgeted on the pew's seat, I blurted out, "Why doesn't Jesus ever come out to play with me?"

She replied, "He does every day. You just have to find him."

Those words began a lifelong search for a God of disguise and surprise and continue to influence my spiritual practices. Over the years, I've discovered that God comes unexpectedly. "God is like that worm you found under the rock and used for fishing bait," my mother once told me in my early teens. "He loves to hide and surprise," she added.

Such experiences as well as teachings about what makes God "happy" or "sad" all influence our earliest God image. I often say that this childhood God gets absorbed into our spiritual DNA and becomes our default image, especially in difficult and trying times as adults.

Our various Christian denominations and Sunday worship sometimes reinforce, sometimes clarify, this image. Songs about God's mercy, grace, love, the need to be prepared for the Day of Judgment, divine concern for the poor and downtrodden, and the gifts of the Creator—all affect how we think about God. Sermons too have their effect: words about God's wrath or the divine desire for prayer, fasting, almsgiving, gratitude, and charity—all add detail to our image of God.

Culture also influences how we think about God. Some cultures in the East (for example, Chinese) emphasize divine transcendence, while others in the West (for example, Italian) delight in the closeness of God. Charlotte's image of God was clearly influenced by her strict Irish upbringing with its traditional emphasis on duty and compliance. Cultures traditionally viewed as primitive are more holistic and apt to see God intertwined in nature as well as in the daily and mundane;

cultures considered as advanced often have a firm division between
the sacred and the secular. Patriarchal cultures tend to stress divine
authority, while matriarchal cultures stress the approachability and
affection of the heavenly.

> **Our idea of God tells us more about ourselves than about Him.**
> Thomas Merton

The portrayal of God by an artist betrays the artist's understanding
of God and can sometimes chisel details into our own image of
God. Sculptures such as Rodin's *The Hand of God* remind us that
God creates life. Paintings such as Rembrandt's *The Return of the
Prodigal Son*, with its depiction of a welcoming father having a
masculine left hand and a feminine right hand, indicate that God is
beyond our understanding of male and female. Handel's "Hallelujah
Chorus" from *The Messiah* celebrates the triumphal power of God.
Gerard Manley Hopkins's "God's Grandeur" is a sonnet describing
God's presence in the natural world. William P. Young's controversial
and bestselling novel *The Shack* depicts the persons of the Trinity
in human form: the Father as an African American woman, the Son
as a Middle-Eastern carpenter, and the Spirit as a wispy Asian woman.

Added to all these influences is the casual language we use to
refer to God. Some people use the masculine pronoun for God;
others like to refer to the Spirit as feminine; still others avoid all
pronouns and simply speak of "God" and "Godself." References to
titles such as the Higher Power, the Supreme Being, the Boss Upstairs, and the Big Man in the Sky betray thoughts about God.

GOD IMAGE CHALLENGED

The very factors that shape our image of God can also challenge
and threaten it. How many times have I heard a spiritual directee,

after hearing a sermon or reading a book or visiting a museum, tell me, "That's not the God I've come to know." This can create discomfort and emotional tension, especially if we are as invested in our God image as Charlotte is, and we usually are.

An experience of tragedy or spiritual darkness can also test how we think about God. On the evening of October 1, 2017, Stephen Paddock opened fire on an outdoor country music festival from the thirty-second floor of the Las Vegas Mandalay Bay resort and casino. More than fifty people died and five hundred were wounded. The following morning, as Americans woke up to the news, I was interviewed about the incident on a national religious talk-radio show.

After introducing me, the host immediately asked, "So, Father, let's get right down to brass tacks. Why did God allow this to happen? I know some people call Vegas 'Sin City,' but is it really *that* terrible? Is God trying to shake us up and get our attention?"

I was speechless. *Does the host really think God was involved with this?* I wondered. Just the thought sent chills down my spine. Repeating what I've heard on many occasions in spiritual direction, I said to myself, *That's not the God I've come to know.*

Gathering my thoughts as best I could on the spur of the moment, I replied, "I certainly don't want to pin this in any way, shape, or form on our loving God. This senseless tragedy is the work of a mentally ill person or someone with a sick, criminal mind. If nothing else, this tragedy tests my belief in the goodness and love of God. I'm sure God is crying over the dead and wounded. But this tragedy also shows me how God surprisingly inspired many first responders and concert goers to risk their lives in helping those who had fallen."

While the Las Vegas shooting seemingly confirmed the host's image of God, it challenged my God image and made me consider again how best, in light of human suffering and tragedy, to think of the ineffable, personal mystery of unconditional love whom we call God.

INADEQUATE GOD IMAGES

Writing about the doctrine of the Trinity, Ronald Rolheiser reminds us of an important fact about God. "God, by definition," he writes, "is ineffable, beyond conceptualization, beyond imagination, beyond language. . . . No formula can ever capture the reality of God because God is too rich to ever be captured, even half adequately, in imagination, thought, and word."

As human beings, we need verbal descriptions and visual images of God. Scripture rightly speaks of God as a creator, a king, a woman in labor, a potter, the protector, a midwife, a fortress, a rock, a nursing mother, a refuge, the deliverer, a lover, the vine grower, and the good shepherd. We would be lost in a meaningless void without these descriptions and images. Like any other one-dimensional photograph, they give us an impression and sometimes even insights into the divine reality.

> God is a great underground river that no one can dam up and no one can stop.
>
> *Meister Eckhart*

However, all descriptions and images—both scriptural and others—are always inadequate and incomplete; they defy rather than define, elude rather than elucidate the fullness of God. We cannot catch God in our descriptions as if God were a butterfly, or capture God in our photographs as if God were a sunset. They betray us when we think we have. Augustine of Hippo states it this way: "*Si comprehendis, non est Deus*" ["If you understand it, it is not God"]. Art, language, and even theology are straitjackets before "the inexpressible, the incomprehensible, the invisible, the un-graspable," personal mystery of unconditional love we call God.

Unfortunately, like Charlotte, we become too emotionally attached to these straitjackets. We idolize the very thing that constricts, and we balk whenever our image of God is questioned, tested, or threatened. When we are unwilling to have our thoughts about God challenged and expanded, we risk losing our direction and being stuck in a pharisaical, cosmetic spirituality that not only fixates on externals but also cripples our adult spiritual formation. That was fifty-five-year-old Charlotte's predicament.

We outgrow our images of God like we outgrow our toys and clothes. Or at least we should. That's normal, natural, and even necessary. As our thoughts about God develop and enlarge through life experience and being challenged, our God image becomes capable of holding the tension found in life's contradictions: the reality of suffering and God's unconditional love; justice deserved and divine mercy rendered; the abundance of sin and the lavishness of grace. Healthy images of God flower in the midst of life's paradoxes and mysteries.

Rozanne goes to church regularly, prays daily, and tries to read her Bible two or three times a week. When asked, she described God as "Someone I can count on to be there to listen to my worries and concerns. He always points me in the right direction. If I get off track, he's quick to take my hand and bring me back. And when I fall, he picks me up."

My heart broke when I heard she lost everything in a tornado that touched down in Joplin, Missouri, in 2011. After a few days, I managed to make contact with her.

"Rozanne, I am so sorry for your loss. I just don't know what to say."

"There's nothing to say. You can rarely predict a natural disaster. All I know is that God is still with me and he'll help Robert and me rebuild. Father, we've lost *everything* we had but the most important: our faith in God. I don't know where I would turn or what I would do if I didn't have God."

In the aftermath of destruction, Rozanne's spiritual maturity and ordinary mysticism shimmered and shone. She again reminded me: a healthy image of God can not only endure a tornado but also provide shelter when your home is in ruins.

How do I know if my image of God is unhealthy?

Unhealthy God images typically inspire fear and dread. Like Charlotte's, they portray God as oppressive, stern, miserly, picayune, uncaring, unloving, and demanding strict obedience. They depict God as wanting to shake us up. They point to ourselves and keep us mindful of our sins instead of God's ardent longing and enthusiastic invitation to a deeper relationship; they make us scrupulous and self-conscious about our thoughts and actions while driving us to obsess over perfection.

Also unhealthy are thoughts about God as an amorphous energy force or something like a Wi-Fi signal with no personal, loving, ardent longing for us. These images are directionless. They do not elicit any inspiration or consolation and typically leave us emotionally flat, sometimes disinterested, and usually apathetic toward the sorrows and tragedies of the world.

Healing such images or outgrowing them takes time, determination, patience, and grace. Because an unhealthy image of God is sometimes rooted in trauma or tragedy, don't be surprised if you need to seek out counseling or therapy. That's what I did to work through the guilt of disrespecting my father a week before he died by suicide. Dealing with my guilt and grief over the loss of my father helped me to get well emotionally. Only then was I in a position to take a look at the compass for my spiritual journey and ask whether God was as distant, stoic, and unmoved by my father's struggles as I had thought.

A JESUS-INSPIRED LIFE COMPASS

Changing deeply ingrained thoughts about God requires awareness and acceptance of the teachings of Jesus. He himself alluded to a number of healthy comparisons for God: a provider (Luke 12:22-31), a shepherd (Luke 15:3-7), a vine grower (John 15:1-2), a welcoming father (Luke 15:11-32), a diligent woman (Luke 15:8-10), an almsgiver (John 6:32-33), a party thrower (Luke 14:15-24), an eraser of debts for those who forgive (Matthew 18:23-35). Each of these images offers a ray of insight into the multifaceted, personal mystery of unconditional love Jesus revealed to us and called "Abba, Father." These images all point to a God with an ardent longing to be in a deeper relationship with us.

Here's one way to help reorient your life compass and have a Jesus-inspired image of God.

Draw a circle on a blank piece of paper. Divide it into four quadrants. Imagine those quadrants as the four cardinal directions, symbolic of the omnipresent, divine presence in whom you live and move and have your being (see Acts 17:28).

Randomly or deliberately choose four of the eight above-mentioned images that Jesus used for God and label one quadrant with each.

At the center of the circle where the four quadrants meet, mark the present moment and your attentive presence to it.

Become mindful of how you got here. Spend time reflecting on the timeline of your life. Note important events such as celebrations, tragedies, dark nights, and moments of mystery. Depending on the four Jesus-inspired images you chose, ask yourself the appropriate following questions:

- As a *provider*, when did God take care of my critical needs? When and how did God encourage me to leave the future with its worries and anxieties and come back to the sacrament of the present moment?

- As a *shepherd*, when and how did God guide me in the right direction? How did he seek me out when I went astray? How has he protected me from the wolves of life?

- As a *vine grower*, when and how did God prune me and challenge me to accept a disappointment? When and how did God strengthen me to endure a tragedy?

- As a *welcoming father*, when and how did God surprise me with a hospitable response to my petition or with careful attention to the details of my situation? When and how has God welcomed me and celebrated my presence with him?

- As a *diligent woman*, when and how did God go out of her way to notice me? To find me?

- As an *almsgiver*, when and how did God respond to my request for help? When and how has God surprised me with generous gifts?

- As a *party thrower*, when and how did God insist I accept his invitation to celebrate an event and feast on its abundance?

- As an *eraser of debts*, when and how has God challenged me to leave the past with its guilt and come back to the sacrament of the present moment? When and how did God lavish on me forgiveness, mercy, and compassion? When and how did God challenge me to forgive himself, myself, or others?

As you ponder the answers to the four appropriate questions, consider writing a specific, personalized short prayer in each quadrant that recognizes, praises, and celebrates God as your chosen Jesus-inspired image. These four written prayers will validate not only God's abiding presence with you but also your mystical awareness.

As you consider each chosen image's questions and write a short prayer, you'll begin to notice how God sometimes showed an ardent longing for you and offered an enthusiastic invitation to a deeper relationship. This mystical mindfulness, born from your own experience, often shapes an understanding of God that is different from your default childhood God or current image of God. This emerging image is often more personal and engaging. Discussing it with a spiritual director or trusted spiritual companion can help you accept, embrace, and celebrate it. As you do, a transformation begins. This Jesus-inspired image of God

- heals your fixation with self-concern by evoking an abiding feeling of safety and security, because God, who feeds the birds and provides for the lilies, is even more invested in you;

- instills a confidence that God, like a shepherd who leaves the flock to search for one lost sheep, has never given up on you no matter how lost you might have felt in the scandal and horror of your sin;

- moves you beyond any preoccupation with self-gratification as it calls forth heroic surrender, sacrifice, and service because God, like a vine grower, prunes fruit-bearing branches to produce even more fruit;

- pulls the plug on the ego's obsession with self-image by stirring up wonder, awe, and gratitude with the realization that the divine unconditional love of the Father makes the sun shine on

the evil and the good and sends rain on the righteous and
the unrighteous;

- makes you feel noticed and counted, because God is like a
  diligent woman meticulously looking for a lost coin;

- alleviates your worries and fears about self-preservation by
  being a divine almsgiver who provides true bread from heaven;

- overlooks your unworthiness and, like a lavish party thrower,
  insists you enjoy a sumptuous banquet; and

- soothes you with compassion for your well-being by refusing
  to allow a debt to stand.

The events of your life witness to a God who is lovingly concerned,
caringly involved, and has an ardent longing for a deeper relationship
with you. This new, healthier image of God validates, comforts, and
inspires; it calls forth your very best as it moves you from a pharisaical and cosmetic spirituality to the cardiac spirituality of Jesus.
You find your apprehensions, fears, and worries decreasing. The
emotional investment in your reputation and what people think of
you slackens and lessens. You no longer fear pain, blame, criticism,
disgrace, or loss. Gratitude and thanksgiving become second-nature
as you see the many and surprising ways God cares and provides.
This Jesus-inspired image of God facilitates the dissipation of the
ego's fixation with self-concern, self-image, self-gratification, and
self-preservation while it reorients the direction in which you
are heading.

And this won't be the last time you'll look at your compass, re-
fashion your image of God, and change your direction. You'll do it
time and again until you finally arrive at the eternal oasis with all
the saints who gaze upon God face-to-face.

Practice

Spend one hour reorienting your life compass and being open to a Jesus-inspired image of God. Ponder the four appropriate questions and write four prayers.

How did this practice challenge your current image of God? How does it challenge your ego obsessions?

Reflect

1. What was the earliest image of God you were given as a compass? Where did it lead you? How often do you revert to it?

2. How has your image of God changed over the years? How does your current image of God hold the tension of life's contradictions and mysteries?

Ponder

A Jesus-inspired image of God is a trusted compass that points an ordinary mystic to the oasis of eternal freedom.

Chapter 10

LIFE, WORDS, SILENCE, AND ACTION

THE SURPRISE OF MYSTICAL PRAYER

*I*n the summer of 1981 as I prepared to make my lifelong commitment to the Franciscan Order—called "solemn vows" of poverty, chastity, and obedience—I made a thirty-day retreat at the Abbey of Gethsemani, the famous Trappist monastery in Kentucky that was home to the late Thomas Merton. I arranged to meet every other day for thirty minutes with an elderly monk.

Don't be surprised: within the first week, I asked this "professional pray-er" for advice about his daily occupation.

"Father," I said, "my prayer is flat and dull and all over the place. I'm not sure what I'm doing wrong. Every time I sit down to pray, I can't seem to keep my attention on God because I am riddled with a barrage of distractions that pull me this way and that. I worry about a friend's sickness. I fantasize about the end of this retreat. I wonder if someone at my friary is collecting my mail. I try to predict tomorrow's weather and fret over next semester's coursework. My prayer is like a cacophony of chaotic concerns that ricochet across my mind. I fidget and fuss as I try my very best to push these thoughts away—but they keep returning. I sometimes think I have a case of *spiritual attention deficit disorder*. What am I supposed to do?"

"Why do you think distractions are such a bad thing?" the Trappist monk asked. "Like any other conversation with a dear friend," he continued, "we all get side-tracked and off-topic from time to time. Don't try to rid your mind of all thoughts and attain a state of thoughtless consciousness—that's not prayer. To try and do that simply becomes another distraction and a source of struggle. Pay attention to your distractions—they're a part of your life right here, right now—and see what they are telling you."

This wise monk reminded me that distractions are normal and, more importantly, are sometimes neon arrows pointing elsewhere: to the need for more rest and relaxation; to an important area of concern; to an aspect of one's personality that needs to be embraced and integrated; to the obligation to communicate with someone; to a minor matter that might need immediate or forthcoming attention. The best way to deal with distractions is to acknowledge them—don't ignore them. Tip your hat to them and discern what they are telling you in the present moment. If it's nothing important and urgent, you can let them go; if it's something important and urgent, you've been informed. That attention can bring deeper knowledge of the self and of God's myriad ways of communicating.

A DIALOGUE

"*Don't try to rid your mind of all thoughts and attain a state of thoughtless consciousness—that's not prayer.*" I still remember those words almost forty years later. And I must confess, I've repeated them time and again to spiritual directees. I sometimes wonder if we've been sold a bill of goods about mystical prayer. We've been told and taught that it is about the ecstatic, the esoteric, or the otherworldly and exists in a hermetically sealed container, disassociated from our lived reality. It's supposed to lift us up to a rarefied space where ineffable secrets are communicated (see 2 Corinthians 12:2-4). Google "Ecstasy of Saint Teresa, Cornaro Chapel, Santa Maria della Vittoria, Rome" to see Bernini's famous statue that depicts this belief.

> For mental prayer, in my opinion, is nothing else than an intimate sharing between friends; it means taking time frequently to be alone with Him whom we know loves us.
>
> Teresa of Avila

Authentic Christian mystical prayer is not about manufacturing pure consciousness with no thoughts or achieving a mind with no distractions. It is not a magic carpet ride to the ethereal. Nor is it a soliloquy. It is a conversation that encourages us to share with God everything about our lives—our thoughts, struggles, joys, sorrows, and concerns about ourselves, our family and friends, and the world. Having shared what's in and on our hearts—even those emotions and feelings we consider inappropriate to show God—we allow time in silence for God to respond. And God does, by not only offering us insights and creative thoughts but also tweaking our feelings and deepest emotions.

As a fourteen-year-old, I was attracted to prayer but didn't know how to begin the conversation. Thankfully, a high school teacher of mine, Fr. Murray, introduced me to a simple method that started my journey. "I call it the 'Come as You Are' prayer," he told me.

He taught me to get into a comfortable but alert sitting position and take a few deep breaths. "Call to mind that God is sitting right across from you. Ask yourself, *What's going on in my life right now? How do I feel about it?* Then tell God your thoughts and feelings," he said. "And then listen for God's response."

When I asked how I would know God is talking, he said, "You'll know God is responding when you feel peace in the midst of a struggle—that's God's way of saying 'Don't worry.' Maybe you suddenly come to a new understanding of someone who hurt your feelings or discover a whole new perspective on a situation. Maybe you have a sudden urge to contact someone by phone. Maybe an idea pops into your head that will help solve your problem. Listen to your thoughts and feelings because that's where God will be replying."

When I mentioned to Fr. Murray that God knows everything I am going to say even before I say it, he replied, "You're absolutely right. You're not giving God any new information. But, as you talk to God about your life and then leave time for him to respond, you'll gradually come to know more about yourself and sometimes even God."

Almost fifty years later, I continue to begin my prayer time with Fr. Murray's "Come as You Are" prayer. In this mindful conversation with God, I've discovered that sometimes I am too desirous and fixated on the gifts of God rather than the Giver. I've experienced how God's ardent longing continues to touch me in times of consolation. I've learned that Jesus enthusiastically invites me to a deeper relationship not only in moments of mystery but also in the storms of life. And in times of darkness, I am reminded that God is not always present in dramatic displays perceived by the senses but, as once happened in the life of Elijah, in "a sound of sheer silence" (1 Kings 19:12).

PRAISE, ADORATION, AND PETITION

As I pray the "Come as You Are" prayer, I am sometimes moved by the sheer reality of God, by God's ardent longing for me, by God's enthusiastic invitation to a deeper relationship expressed through creation, family members, friends, the present moment's unmet need or required duty, and most of all, in the divine experience called human love. Praise and adoration are mindful ways to respond to these expressions of God. Google "The Ecstasy of St. Francis, Bellini" to see the fifteenth-century painter's famous rendition of such a moment. Some denominations express praise and adoration liturgically; others express them in singing praise and worship songs. The ritual of praying grace before and after meals is another way of being mindful and responding to God; Norman Rockwell captured just this moment in his painting, *Saying Grace.*

My friends Marie and Blaise have expanded my vision of prayer. While breastfeeding her newborn, Marie is often moved to adoration of the Author of Life and whispers, "Can a woman forget her nursing child, or show no compassion for the child of her womb? Even these may forget, yet I will not forget you" (Isaiah 49:15). Getting his hands dirty and planting his garden, Blaise is mindful of the divine creativity he discovers in the flowering birds of paradise, bluebonnets, bougainvilleas, and buttercups. In the cathedral of life, nature provides the stained-glass windows inspiring many an ordinary mystic to kneel in wonder and awe.

Sometimes I come to prayer very much aware that I am a beggar: I have needs, wishes, and desires. Sometimes they are focused on me. Sometimes others. And still other times, the world. The "Come as You Are" prayer includes petition and intercession.

"When people ask me to pray for them, I take it seriously. I keep a running list of people and their petitions for which I pray every day. But I don't seem to have much luck. Most of my petitions go unanswered—and that sometimes discourages me. What's the secret to intercessory prayer?" Tracy's face betrayed bewilderment.

I reminded her that intercessory prayers are not like a rain dance that, if done properly and often, will make the skies open up. Nor are they a way of strong-arming God to get what we want. Rather, petitionary and intercessory prayers are another way of responding to the unmet need or required duty of the present moment. *Who do I need to think of and pray for today?* is a great question to answer as we continue the conversation with God. *Please help Betty get a clean bill of health. Inspire Philip as he takes his final exam.* Petition and intercession help deepen our relationships with others and strengthen our cardiac spirituality.

It took me a while to come to an appreciation for prayers of petition and intercession. I owe that again to Fr. Murray. After I had become comfortable with his "Come as You Are" prayer, he encouraged me to lengthen my prayer time with Scripture or a text from a classic or contemporary spiritual writer. I would slowly read a few verses or a paragraph. I then would pause and think about what I had just read. This pondering would last for a couple of minutes. Once I had received as much as I could, I would return to the text, read a few more lines, and then ponder again.

After a few months, Fr. Murray suggested I ask three important questions that became part of my spiritual reading: *What did the passage or text tell me about God's relationship with me? How did that knowledge touch my heart and move me? How should my thoughts, words, and actions change as a result of that passage?* By answering these three questions, I found ways to make the words on the page come alive and have an effect on me. That sometimes led me to pray for specific needs or virtues. My petitions initially were focused on myself.

My appreciation for intercessory prayer's wider vision didn't really flower until Fr. Murray coached me in another simple method of prayer: praying the news.

"Watch the evening news," he said, "or read the daily newspaper. As you do, become aware of how you are responding to the news story. If a particular story touches you deeply, then bring it to prayer and tell God about it."

Praying the news continues to be a part of my daily practice. It's another way to respond to the present moment's unmet need or required duty not only in faraway places but also in situations where my inability to help is painfully apparent.

THE ENTIRE HUMAN DIMENSION

Authentic Christian mystical prayer is never disassociated from our lived reality—we pray from where we are, not from where we think we should be. It embraces every dimension of the human condition: physical, mental, spiritual, and social. Think of Jesus giving sight to a man born blind (John 9:1-41), healing the mental illness of the Gerasene demoniac (Mark 5:1-20), freeing people from spiritual demons (Luke 8:2), and restoring a leper to his social circle of relationships (Matthew 8:1-4). This has three important implications for the ordinary mystic.

> Praying is no easy matter. It demands a relationship in which you allow someone other than yourself to enter into the very center of your person, to see there what you would rather leave in darkness, and to touch there what you would rather leave untouched.
>
> Henri Nouwen

Everything is appropriate to bring before God. Nothing needs to be excluded. Anything that is a source of joy, shame, fear, worry, anger, or confusion—trivial or unseemly as it may be—finds expression in an ordinary mystic's prayer. This requires honesty as a multitude of feelings and needs arise and are expressed: the tickled satisfaction of capturing a special moment in a photograph; the guilt associated with a recurring sin; the anguish of encountering a child with cancer; a prayer to help make ends meet; the soulful exuberance of listening to a favorite song; the hope to live long enough to see a daughter's wedding. Any technique or method that promotes transparency, a hallmark of authentic Christian mystical prayer, is the best way to pray.

Second, transparency in prayer is not confined to the spoken word. It can be expressed in many other ways. Think of David dancing before the Lord "with all his might" (2 Samuel 6:14) or the guilt-ridden woman bathing the feet of Jesus with her tears and drying them with her hair (Luke 7:36-50). Eastern Christianity has the tradition of writing icons. "*Qui cantat,*" wrote Augustine of Hippo, "*bis orat*" ["The one who sings, prays twice"]. Different cathedrals around the world have been referred to as prayers in stone. Artists plumb the depths of human experience and pray in dance, floral arrangements, music, paint, pantomime, photography, and poetry.

Finally, there is a social dimension to prayer that not only includes intercession but also goes beyond it. "But I say to you, love your enemies and pray for those who persecute you" (Matthew 5:44). "And forgive us our sins, for we ourselves forgive everyone indebted to us" (Luke 11:4). "So when you are offering your gift at the altar, if you remember that your brother or sister has something against you, leave your gift there before the altar and go; first be reconciled to your brother or sister, and then come and offer your gift" (Matthew 5:23-24). Mystical prayer has an effect on the way we live: it strengthens our familial bonds and drives us into more honest, transparent relationships by fostering Jesus' cardiac spirituality of surrender, sacrifice, and service.

BOTH INDIVIDUAL AND COMMUNAL

The personalities of ordinary mystics determine the different ways of praying that interest or attract them. Some extroverts like vocal prayer. Some introverts are drawn to meditation. There is no one method that necessarily satisfies everyone. One challenge on the spiritual journey is to find what prayer techniques are nourishing and helpful in responding to God's ardent longing and enthusiastic invitation to a deeper relationship.

Over the years, I've noticed times when my prayer was hopelessly flat. The techniques and methods were burdensome. *Why isn't this working any longer?* I asked. The temptation to quit or take a vacation from prayer was very real. On many occasions I've had a niggling thought that I was doing something wrong or praying incorrectly.

"Don't be foolish. You're doing nothing wrong," a spiritual director once told me. "There's no 'wrong way' to pray except when you doggedly hang on to a technique or method that no longer satisfies or when you simply pray by rote. Or even worse, when you stop being honest and transparent with God."

It's quite common to outgrow prayer techniques or even change methods due to our circumstances or situation. Like a GPS tracker, our prayer should adjust and recalculate as we grow in mindfulness and respond to God's longing and invitation. Mystical prayer breathes, develops, changes course, and grows with each season of life. It is never set in stone.

A charming Franciscan legend about Saints Francis and Clare illustrates another facet of mystical prayer. Francis had continually turned down Clare's request to share a meal. After the prodding of the friars, he finally agreed. A meeting and meal were arranged at the little church of St. Mary of the Angels located in the woods down in the valley.

At the appointed hour, the future saints, each with companions, met and sat on the ground. As they shared a meal of simple fare, Francis began to speak about spiritual things in such a marvelous way that he himself, Clare, and the companions were caught up in God.

Meanwhile, horror seized the citizens of Assisi as they watched the little church and the entire forest around it go up in flames. The citizens rushed down the hill with buckets of water and hearts spilling over with the hope of extinguishing the fire. Upon arrival at the church, they found Francis, Clare, and the companions rapt in mystical ecstasy.

There was no fire. The blaze the people saw was the love of God burning in the lives of these simple followers of Christ.

The legend reminds us that mystical prayer can also be communal. Worship services, liturgies, prayer groups, and the Liturgy of the Hours—a fixed-hour prayer of the Psalms typically recited in community—are also ways we grow in our relationships with God and others. There is a sacramental quality about communal prayer: "For where two or three are gathered in my name, I am there among them" (Matthew 18:20). Ideally, private prayer should lead to communal prayer and communal prayer should fuel our private prayer. The God discovered in the "Come as You Are" prayer is the same God worshiped in community. That rhythm of bringing private prayer to community prayer, and reflecting privately on what we hear and experience in community prayer, can help promote transparency.

NOT JUST WORDS BUT THE SILENCE BETWEEN THEM

Over time, I noticed I was becoming weary with words and more attracted to silence. I was moved to simply bask in God's presence with wordless, mindful wonder. Was that still prayer?

"Yes, that's still prayer, and it's typical for anyone who prays every day to finally arrive there," my spiritual director told me. "Prayer is about honesty, and we should never cling to words just to fill in the gaps. That's when methods and techniques get in the way and hinder our spiritual growth. Jesus himself challenged us not to prattle on like the pagans (see Matthew 6:7). Stirring up more words or trying to manufacture uplifting emotions do not get us a special hearing from God.

"The psalmist says, 'Be still, and know that I am God' (Psalm 46:10), so follow the silence when you are so moved. Use that verse from Psalm 46, some other short verse from Scripture, or a prayer word. Recite it slowly and deliberately. Coordinate it with your breathing. When moved, let the verse or prayer word go and sit in the silence made holy by God's presence. When the silence flames out or you catch yourself chasing distractions as inevitably and quickly happens, come back to the holy silence by repeating the verse or prayer word. Then follow the silence again until you get sidetracked and need to return to it with the verse or word. This becomes like a slow dance of prayer, silence, prayer, silence."

When my spiritual director mentioned this to me, I was reminded that sometimes the most honest and transparent dialogue between lovers is the silence of a loving glance. That silence is not a hollow moment vacant of words; it is a prolonged pause pregnant with passion. Growth in mystical prayer is growth in loving silence.

> Do not be too anxious about your advancement in the ways of prayer because you have left the beaten track and are traveling by paths that cannot be charted and measured. Therefore leave God to take care of your degree of sanctity and contemplation. If you yourself try to measure your own progress you will waste your time in futile introspection.
>
> *Thomas Merton*

Tasting silence and basking in the wordless love of God during prayer was extraordinarily satisfying. I was confident I was on the right track and still remember thinking, *Now I'm making progress.* I proudly suspected I was in the foothills of mystical prayer.

It's a common temptation for us to look in the mirror and become focused, self-absorbed, and overly concerned about progress in prayer. It's a common misconception (and part of the bill of goods we were sold about mysticism) to think of prayer as a pathway to experiences: from words to feelings of peace and joy to silence to mystical ecstasy. We commonly judge the quality of our prayer on such fruits—but prayer cannot be confined to an interior journey where we collect feelings and experiences as if they were souvenirs. More important, it is an interior journey that must find expression beyond ourselves, in the two-fold love of God and neighbor that is the hallmark of the ordinary mystic (the English word *ecstasy* is derived from the Greek *ekstasis*, "to stand outside oneself").

Authentic Christian mystical prayer goes beyond the cosmetic, gets underneath the skin, and opens up the heart. It ever so gradually aligns the longings of the heart with the longing of God. This alignment not only deflates the ego with its four obsessions but also moves beyond mere behavior modification, uniting the human will to God's. This culminates in the highest form of mystical prayer, "Thy will be done." This loving stance of surrender, sacrifice, and service is the response to the present moment's unmet need or required duty. It is the essence of Jesus' cardiac spirituality: "For I have come down from heaven, not to do my own will, but the will of him who sent me" (John 6:38). It transforms the very presence of the person into a prayer itself—into an ordinary mystic.

Ordinary mystics are mindful of this world, their lives, and the present moment. They intercede for the crises, needs, and hardships of the world. They petition for personal requests. But most of all, they celebrate in life, word, silence, and action God's ardent longing and enthusiastic invitation to a deeper relationship right here, right now.

Practice

Practice the "Come as You Are" prayer for one week.

After a week, assess its fruitfulness in your life.

What has it taught you about mindfulness and the presence of God?

Reflect

1. How often do you look in the mirror to check your spiritual progress? What help or hindrance has that knowledge been to you?

2. Reflect on the history of your prayer life. How has your prayer life changed over the years? What has your experience taught you about progress in prayer?

Ponder

The hallmark of mystical prayer is mindfulness, transparency, and the desire to do God's will right here, right now.

Chapter 11

EARS TO THE GROUND

LISTENING TO GOD

*D*aniel prays every day. Part of his prayer time is pondering the Gospel from that day's Mass lectionary. One day, the reading was about Jesus calling his first disciples. These words seemed to jump off the page: "Follow me, and I will make you fish for people" (Matthew 4:19). That verse lingered with Daniel for several days.

A month earlier, Daniel's pastor had approached him. "The archdiocese is soon training a new class of permanent deacons. It's a five-year program that includes academic study and a ministerial commitment. I think you are an ideal candidate. The program leaders also ask the wives to attend the classes and play an active role in the training. Would you talk to Regina and see if this is something both of you would be interested in?"

Daniel suspected a connection between these two events and brought it to me for his monthly spiritual direction session. "I don't think it's a coincidence. I didn't know why that verse struck me until

I remembered what Fr. Gallagher had asked me a couple of weeks ago. I'm wondering if God is trying to tell me something."

How do you discern a coincidence from a nudging from God? Are they one and the same? How do you know the difference between the voice of God and your imagination? How does God use people and events to influence your life? Are gut feelings and inclinations trustworthy indicators of God's will? Discernment is one of the fundamental challenges in the spiritual life and mindfulness is an important component of its practice. Both require knowledge of the ways of God.

YOUR LIFE AS GOD'S MEGAPHONE

There's a common misconception that God always speaks in an otherworldly manner—that's how we know it's God. Like thunder, his voice booms and comes from the sky. It's occasionally mysterious but always mystical. Sometimes it startles the listener and typically is life changing.

Paul's experience on the road to Damascus is the perfect biblical example. An intense persecutor of the Christians, known as Saul before his conversion, the future apostle was zealous in the traditions of his Jewish faith (Galatians 1:13-14). According to the Acts of the Apostles (see Acts 9:3-9), as he approached Damascus, Saul suddenly encountered a heavenly light that flashed around him. He fell to the ground and heard a voice ask, "Saul, Saul, why do you persecute me?" The risen Christ told him that it was he himself Saul was persecuting. Saul was instructed to get up and go to Damascus where he would receive instructions on what to do. Now blinded, he was led by the hand to Damascus where for three days he did not eat or drink anything.

Ananias received a divine revelation to visit Saul, who was staying in the house of Judas. Initially hesitant because of Saul's reputation, Ananias obeyed the divine command. He placed his hands on Saul and prayed that Saul be filled with the Holy Spirit. Saul's sight returned and he was baptized (Acts 9:13-19). It was a life-changing moment in Saul's life and in Christianity as he was transformed into the apostle to the Gentiles.

> Do not make the mistake of aspiring to the spectacular "experiences" that you read about in the lives of great mystics.
>
> Thomas Merton

The more I walk the spiritual journey, the more I realize that Paul's mystical experience on the road to Damascus is a sideshow in the history of spirituality. So are the experiences of people like Francis of Assisi hearing a voice from the crucifix in the church of San Damiano, Joan of Arc getting instructions from deceased saints, Patrick of Ireland being guided by voices to return to his homeland as a missionary for the Christian faith, Bernadette Soubirous seeing the vision of Mary in a grotto of Lourdes, and many others. Otherworldly, mystical, and impressive as these experiences are, they can easily distract us from the more common ways that God speaks to us.

What are those more common ways? God uses our very lives as a megaphone to communicate with us; that's the major takeaway from Paul's experience on the way to Damascus. Just as mystical prayer embraces every dimension of the human condition—physical, mental, spiritual, and social—so too discernment embraces these same dimensions as the sacred arena where God speaks. Let's briefly explore each of these dimensions and see how mindfulness can aid in the discernment process.

Physical Dimension. God uses our physical surroundings. Things in nature—like September's harvest moon, a bald eagle floating in the sky, an evening breeze as we walk in the heat of summer, a blooming cactus—might bring a reminder of God's abiding presence and longing for us. The frustration we experience at our present job site might be God's challenge to surrender and trust—or to look for different employment. A hand outstretched for alms, a crying infant, or a stranger with a flat tire is God's way of moving us beyond our ego obsessions and deepening our cardiac spirituality of surrender, sacrifice, and service. Intriguing coincidences, such as Daniel experienced with his pastor and Scripture, might be unexpected invitations from God. Our personal history, past and present, might be a stunning testimony to God's grace and fidelity.

I can't remember not wanting to be a missionary to mainland China. The opportunity presented itself in 1992 and off I went, first to the island of Taiwan for two and a half years for language and culture studies, and then to the city of Wuhan to teach English. It was a very difficult year in Wuhan as I adjusted to life on the mainland. I still remember that Sunday morning in November 1995 when I heard on the BBC News that Yitzhak Rabin had been assassinated. That news deepened the depression I was already feeling over my struggles with the Chinese culture. And yet, as I rode the ferry across the Yangtze River to attend Mass at the Hankow cathedral, I saw the Chinese flag flying in the distance and asked myself in wonder, *Am I really here in mainland China?* My depression suddenly lifted as I realized again that I was living my childhood dream. That realization was not only a consolation from God but also a welcomed confirmation of where I was and what I was doing.

Mental Dimension. God can speak through the inner life of the mind. Have you ever been prompted to do something that seemingly came out of nowhere and turned out to be exactly what needed to be done? Ever have a hunch or intuition that turned out to be spot-on? God sometimes nudges us to action through thoughts that seemingly come out of nowhere.

God sometimes uses our imagination to heal us of childhood trauma, to enthusiastically invite us to a deeper relationship, or to strengthen our resolve for a particular task. God has spoken to many people as they pray a form of imaginative prayer in which they place themselves in a Gospel scene and sense their reactions to Jesus' ministry. Even dreams, as a manifestation of the unconscious and correctly interpreted, can offer insights into our present situation or an impending decision. Though some people disparage such communications as being of their own making, the fact is: God can and does speak to us by directing our thoughts and using our minds.

Recently, while brushing my teeth, the thought crossed my mind that I hadn't talked to my good friend Fr. Tom in more than five months. I had heard his health had taken a turn for the worse, and I told myself to call him. But I didn't.

Two days later, as I got out of bed at 5 a.m., the thought returned —but this time with more conviction. I immediately wrote myself a note to call him that afternoon. Ninety minutes later that very morning, I received a phone call. "Albert, I am sorry for calling so early but I wanted you to be the first to know that Tom was found dead this morning. He died in his sleep." I am convinced two days earlier God had offered me an opportunity to talk to my dear friend.

Spiritual Dimension. Many of us are familiar with the way God speaks through our commitment to spiritual formation. The Old Testament aligns our lives with the Ten Commandments and God's covenant. In the Sermon on the Mount, Jesus, God's saving Word made flesh, stretches us to a cardiac spirituality of surrender, sacrifice, and service. The letters of the New Testament offer us insights into living as a community of believers saved through God's ardent longing for us. The book of Revelation offers hope in times of persecution. Sacred tradition, through the help of the Holy Spirit, teaches us how to interpret and give flesh to God's Word in our contemporary world. The church, as a community of believers, offers us encouragement by reminding us that we are family; her sacraments offer us unique encounters with God. In worship services, God touches us through sermons and hymns. And in personal prayer, God calls us to our vocations, confronts our ego obsessions, challenges our desires, consoles us in difficult times, and confides confidence in us.

Fr. Tom's sister, Rosie, was heartbroken over her brother's death. We grieved together at his wake service and funeral. She sobbed as I left for my return flight to Texas. Two weeks later, she telephoned me. "I miss Tom so much," she said. "He was such a source of strength and inspiration for me. But as I was praying the other day," she continued, "the thought struck me that he's in a better place now. A feeling came over me that everything is going to be okay. God is with me even in my sadness." God was ministering to Rosie in her prayer.

Social Dimension. God speaks to us through our relationships and social commitments: "For where two or three are gathered in my name, I am there among them" (Matthew 18:20). God calls some people to the single life through their commitments to family and friends; God calls some people to marriage by sending a special person into their lives who sparks the flames of selfless love; God calls still others to ministry or religious life by having a family member, friend, or pastor in Daniel's case, suggest the idea. A coworker's challenging word might be God's way of calling us to repentance; a confidant's pat on the back might be God's encouragement;

a child's joy might be a sign of divine delight; an elderly parent's lingering amid an incurable disease might be God's way of offering extra time for reconciliation.

God speaks to us day in, day out, through the human dimensions of our everyday routine and humdrum lives. Our challenge is to be attentive to this divine voice, discern its message and meaning right here, right now, and then respond in an appropriate manner. "Thy will be done." The mundane and ordinary is charged with the mystical and otherworldly for those who live with mindfulness.

Practice

Choose one dimension of your life: physical, mental, spiritual, or social. Call to mind what happened in it over the past week.

Having recalled the past week, ask yourself: *How might God have been speaking to me? What might God have been asking of me?*

Reflect

1. What extraordinary spiritual experiences has God given to you? How do you honor them? What did you learn from them?

2. Of the four dimensions of human experience, to which one are you most attuned? Least attuned? How has God recently used either of them to speak to you?

Ponder

Your very life in its four dimensions is the sacred arena where God speaks.

Chapter 12

PRACTICAL PRACTICES

RESPONDING TO GOD

The variety of spiritual practices is daunting. Just off the top of my head, I can instantly name the more common ones I've either tried or have suggested to others: gratitude, sabbath rest, journaling, prayer, silence, solitude, detachment, submission, chastity, hospitality, almsgiving, service, spiritual direction, compassion, humility, fasting, and fixed-hour prayer. Being intentional about spiritual formation, I sometimes am bewildered and discouraged as I ask myself, *Where do I begin with the spiritual disciplines? Which is the best to practice? Why doesn't fasting work for me? How can I practice fixed-hour prayer when my schedule is full or I'm traveling?* I'm embarrassed to admit it: I haven't had much success with practicing many of the traditional disciplines.

In their desire to respond to God's ardent longing and enthusiastic invitation to a deeper relationship, many people have asked me about the purpose and practice of spiritual disciplines. I remember

Dominic saying and asking, "I guess it's like going to the gym and having a workout routine that changes depending on the day of the week. After all, you have to exercise all your muscles to stay in shape. Doesn't soul training require variety, intentionality, and discipline?"

"*Soul training*." I like Dominic's image. And many other people do too. Choosing deliberate external behaviors and backing them up with the thinking of the Sermon on the Mount can form healthy habits; both shape the silhouette of one's soul. The old saying "practice makes perfect" speaks to this point: the more we practice a spiritual discipline and allow our minds to be renewed (see Romans 12:2; Ephesians 4:23), the more we grow in our identity as Christian disciples and ordinary mystics.

"*Soul training*." As much as I like the expression, I do have some reservations about it. It might suggest that spiritual formation is concerned with measurable outcomes and goals reached by spending time on an otherworldly treadmill and lifting religious weights. It might promote the spiritually mature as muscle-builders who oil their bodies, flex their muscles, posture, and pose like the Pharisees demanding places of honor, wearing long showy tassels, and feeling justified in demanding to be called rabbi (Matthew 23:5-7). These people could look proudly in the mirror, be tempted to take personal credit for the shape they're in, and self-righteously pray, "God, I thank you that I am not like other people: thieves, rogues, adulterers, or even like this tax collector. I fast twice a week; I give a tenth of all my income" (Luke 18:11-12). In effect, the image of soul training is not only dangerously close to the Pelagian heresy, which believes all spiritual growth is the result of brute willpower, but also suggestive of a spiritual elitism, a humanly made mysticism.

PRINCIPLES

I like to think of the practice of the disciplines as our response to a spiritual alarm clock that wakes us up and keeps us mindful of the present moment. It's in the present moment that God expresses his ardent longing for us—that's why this very moment is a sacrament and ambassador as mentioned in chapter one—and enthusiastically invites us to a deeper relationship. That invitation often comes in this unmet need or required duty right here, right now. Let's take a look at five principles for practicing spiritual disciplines and see how the disciplines keep us awake and alert to the here and now.

> For often when a person is distracted and forgetful of God, His Majesty will awaken it. His action is as quick as a falling comet. And as clearly as it hears a thunderclap, even though no sound is heard, the soul understands that it was called by God.
>
> *Teresa of Avila*

First, *spiritual disciplines are our response to an experience of God's ardent longing and enthusiastic invitation to a deeper relationship.* The journey begins with God's initiative and invitation. "In this is love, not that we loved God but that he loved us" (1 John 4:10). This experience of grace is an awakening that not only makes us feel noticed but also calls us to action.

This awakening and invitation can happen at any moment. The beginning of Donald's journey provides one example. His college friend had been trying for a number of years to convince Donald to join him on a weekend retreat at a local retreat house. "I was always able to come up with an excuse not to go," he told me in our first spiritual direction session. "But for some reason, this year I decided I would give it a try. After all, it was just one weekend. On Saturday night, I sat in the chapel. I was bored to death and tried to figure out what I was doing there. Suddenly, out of nowhere, this feeling of peace washed over me. It engulfed and stayed with me for the rest of the night and the following morning. And now as I talk about it, my body still remembers it. At the end of the retreat, I realized I needed to get serious about my relationship with God. I told my friend about that chapel experience, and he suggested I might want to get a spiritual director. He told me about you." Donald's awakening started with a palpable experience of God's grace; he responded with the discipline of spiritual direction.

Denise had a very different experience. She sat in shock as her doctor told her she had stage IV cancer. "It has metastasized to your lungs and uterus," the doctor said. "Our challenge is to keep you as comfortable as possible for the next six-to-nine months." Two weeks later, Denise contacted her parish priest. She had spent time examining her life and taking a moral inventory. She wanted to celebrate God's mercy and forgiveness.

Both experiences highlight God's use of surprising and significant incidents as wake-up calls to a deeper relationship. Spiritual disciplines get our feet on the floor and our bodies out of bed.

OPENNESS TO GRACE

Unlike using gym equipment that strengthens our muscles, spiritual disciplines are not transforming in themselves. The transformation occurs as we open ourselves and respond to God's longing and invitation. Spiritual practices facilitate this opening and surrender of the will. Consequently, as the second principle states, *spiritual disciplines should foster mindfulness.* They heighten our awareness of God's abiding grace at ever deepening levels of our lives and of the strategies we employ to sabotage grace's transforming action through our attachment to the four obsessions of the ego.

> The various disciplines of the spiritual life are meant for freedom and are reliable means for the creation of helpful boundaries in our lives within which God's voice can be heard, God's presence felt, and God's guidance experienced.
>
> *Henri Nouwen*

Vivian has always been committed to the practice of her faith. For a fortieth-birthday gift to herself, she decided to attend a weekend journaling workshop sponsored by her church. She had been experiencing elusive interior stirrings and thought this workshop might help her get in touch with what was going on. Practicing different journaling exercises that weekend, Vivian discovered that she needed to be less concerned about other people's opinions and more trusting that God would guide her in the direction she needed to go. Naming that nagging preoccupation and committing herself to a deeper faith in God were a moment of freedom, proving to her the benefits of journaling. As a result, she decided to journal on a weekly basis. Now, two years later, though she rarely rereads her journal's old entries, just sitting at the kitchen table and writing in her journal make her sensitive to both God's action in her life and the obstacles she places in its way.

"THY WILL BE DONE"

Third, *authentic spiritual disciplines facilitate surrender to the will of God.* As we grow in the awareness of God's grace and stay awake with spiritual practices, we are emboldened to respond to the ambassador of the present moment. That ambassador declares the will of God in its unmet need or required duty. And our response? "Thy will be done."

> A saint is a person who when he does his own will, is doing the will of God. . . . The root of his willing is in God. . . . The greatest glory of a creature is to act freely as the instrument of God. . . . His acts are Christ's.
>
> *Thomas Merton*

My friend Cindy is quite intentional about praying daily, fasting weekly, and retreating annually into silence and solitude for an extended weekend. She's been practicing all three for more than a decade. Her heightened sensitivity to God's grace has illumined areas of selfishness and sin. Made aware of them, she's been quite open in discussing these areas with her spiritual director. Those discussions ultimately led to some important decisions that affected her lifestyle: She began volunteering one day a week at her church's food pantry. She started a pen pal relationship with a woman on death row. I still remember the day she called me and said, "My spiritual practices convinced me that God was calling me to feed the hungry and befriend a prisoner. I now consider myself a co-worker for the kingdom." Over time, Cindy's mindfulness revealed her call to mission—and she responded. This is the adventure of spiritual formation, is it not? In the words of Jesus, "Not everyone who says to me, 'Lord, Lord,' will enter the kingdom of heaven, but only the one who does the will of my Father in heaven" (Matthew 7:21).

NOT FOR EVERYONE

My experience with fasting leads to the fourth principle about spiritual disciplines. I'm only too aware of fasting's revered history with firm biblical roots. It emerges in the Old Testament in times of war, sickness, death, impending danger, and guilt (see Judges 20:26; 2 Samuel 1:12, 12:16-23; 2 Chronicles 20:3; Jonah 3:4-10). In the New Testament, Jesus himself promotes the practice; the churches of Antioch and Galatia as well as the apostle Paul fasted (Matthew 6:16-18; Acts 13:1-3; 14:21-23).

Some of the great figures in the history of Christian spirituality have promoted its practice. St. Peter Chrysologus called fasting "the soul of prayer." Saints Benedict, Hildegard of Bingen, Francis of Assisi, Catherine of Siena, Teresa of Avila, Ignatius of Loyola, and others recommended it. Citing Augustine, St. Thomas Aquinas reminded his readers of its spiritual effects: "Fasting cleanses the soul, raises the mind, subjects one's flesh to the spirit, renders the heart contrite and humble, scatters the clouds of concupiscence, quenches the fire of lust, kindles the true light of chastity."

Can you imagine my guilt over the years as I've struggled with fasting? I have white knuckled my way through many a day of fasting only to find myself in the evening irritable and edgy. It certainly has not cleansed my soul, raised my mind, or made me humble. Nor did it heighten my awareness of God's grace or lead me to surrender to God's will. If anything, it kept my thoughts fixated on the following morning's breakfast.

"Fasting from food might not be your cup of tea," Fr. Dan cleverly said as he mixed his metaphors. "It's not for everybody. But there

> We must be careful not to practice a formal fast, or one which in truth "satisfies" us because it makes us feel good about ourselves. Fasting makes sense if it questions our security, and if it also leads to some benefit for others, if it helps us to cultivate the style of the Good Samaritan, who bends down to his brother in need and takes care of him.
>
> *Pope Francis*

are other ways to fast. You can fast from text messages or emails for a day and spend that time helping a neighbor. You can fast from the internet or television and make a phone call to a friend. You can fast from gossip or grudges."

Fourth, *not every traditional practice of a spiritual discipline is helpful for every person.* A person's temperament, physical condition, personality, and religious denomination all play a role in whether a particular spiritual practice is helpful. Just as there is no one prayer technique that is helpful for everyone, so too there is no one way to fast that is helpful for all.

Fr. Dan continued, "You need to find your own way of actively responding to God's grace and deliberately disengaging from egotistical preoccupations—that's really the purpose of fasting. It might include fasting today from concern about your reputation and what people are saying behind your back; fasting from your worries and anxieties; fasting from selfish desires and feelings; or even fasting from saving today's wage for yourself."

If you're like me and the traditional practice of fasting—or any other spiritual discipline—doesn't seem to benefit you, don't worry or think something is wrong with you. Fr. Dan's advice reminded me that each of us is on a unique journey with its own twists and turns; we need to trust that God's grace leads each of us in the direction we need to go. Awareness of that ever-deepening divine invitation and how we decline it comes to some through journaling, to others through prayer and almsgiving, still others through hospitality, gratitude, or service. But your journaling might take the form of doodling or drawing an unnamed feeling; your prayer might be in the context of swimming rather than sitting in silence; your alms might be care and concern rather than currency; your hospitality might be opening your heart rather than your home. Any practice that makes us mindful of God's ardent longing for us and helps us respond to God's invitation is acceptable, because *intentionality is the key component for each and every spiritual discipline.* That's the fifth principle.

Discovering a beneficial way to fast didn't come easily for me. It took some trial and error. After many attempts over the years, I've come up with a few practices. As a way to keep my ego in check, I sometimes spend a week fasting from checking my books' Amazon rankings. During the season of Lent, if I awake one morning hankering for a certain food, I'll abstain from it that day. As an expression of Sabbath rest on Sundays, I typically don't check emails or go online; instead, I spend a bit more time in prayer, sometimes praying over the latest international crisis. On Fridays, the day that Franciscans customarily fast, I specifically pray for those whom I find difficult and try my best to ignore the grudges I harbor against them. Since intentionality is the key component for any spiritual discipline, I'm limited in my approach to fasting only by my creativity.

IN THE SMALLEST AND MOST ORDINARY WAYS

This fifth principle also makes *any* practice a spiritual practice if done with the intention of becoming aware, acknowledging, and acting on God's grace. This is one of my takeaways from the story of the visitation (Luke 1:39-56). Mary, the virgin with child, goes "with haste" (Luke 1:39)—almost as if she is on a mission—to visit her relative Elizabeth. No doubt she is eager to witness to God's miracle not only in her own life but also in the life of her relative who, in her old age, is pregnant with the Precursor. Mary's hymn of praise (Luke 1:47-55) gives expression to a stunning tapestry with gratitude woven into every verse. Mary is testifying to her faith as this simple family visit becomes a proclamation of God's grace at work in her life and the life of the world.

Even the smallest expression of gratitude becomes a spiritual practice when it celebrates and testifies to God's action in our lives. Bringing a loaf of freshly baked bread to a neighbor, sending flowers to a friend, making a phone call to an elderly relative, or writing a thank you note or email, can witness to the thread of God's grace coming into our lives and stitching us to another's. We acknowledge, sometimes with haste, how the other person has been God's instrument in a moment of listening, desperation, mourning, loneliness, or celebration. Grace broadens our vision and is always communal; it is never private and individualistic.

Though the traditional custom of the day would oblige the younger to greet the other, it is elderly Elizabeth, living with keen mindfulness of the present moment, who recognizes the sanctity of such a visit, as the mother of the Lord unexpectedly visits her home. She greets Mary with a salutation that proclaims the virgin's dignity and role in salvation history: "Blessed are you among women, and blessed is the fruit of your womb" (Luke 1:42). Caught up in her own private joy, Elizabeth not only pauses to acknowledge the presence of the other but also offers the younger relative hospitality for three months. This is cardiac spirituality: surrender, sacrifice, and service.

The visitation reveals another simple gesture, besides gratitude, as a spiritual practice. When we attentively prepare the guest room

> Let all guests who arrive be received as Christ, because He will say: "I was a stranger and you took Me in" (Matthew 25:35). And let due honor be shown to all, especially to those "of the household of the faith" (Galatians 6:10) and to wayfarers.
>
> *Rule of St. Benedict*

or lovingly cook a meal or carefully lay the table, we are acknowledging the sacredness of every visit by a relative, friend, neighbor, or foe. Whether planned or unexpected, short or lengthy, each is a divine encounter that surprises us—"And why has this happened to me, that the mother of my Lord comes to me?" (Luke 1:43)—and our response to such a grace is the spiritual practice of hospitality.

PRAYER BEFORE DAWN

Raymond is happily married, the father of three children, and a vice president of a bank. Every Wednesday morning at 4 a.m., his alarm goes off and he gets out of bed. He throws cold water on his face and then spends one hour in prayer. He discovered this practice five years ago while making a retreat at a Trappist monastery. After his hour of prayer, he gets ready for work.

Every Saturday morning, he travels two hours to have lunch with Charlie, his college roommate. Unfortunately, because he suffers from early-onset Alzheimer's disease, Charlie has no idea who this stranger is.

"Can I ask you a question, Raymond?" I once asked. "With so much on your plate—your wife, the children, work, your prayer before dawn every Wednesday morning—why on earth do you sacrifice a major part of your weekend to make a four-hour round-trip to visit someone who doesn't even recognize you?"

Raising an eyebrow with a look of surprise, he simply said, "It's a way for me to extend my Wednesday morning prayer and witness to what I have learned from it: I must forget myself and respond to those in need."

Raymond's reply speaks volumes about the connection between the spiritual practice of prayer and action. For him, prayer before dawn is not simply about a dialogue with God or meditation. It is a spiritual discipline that fosters mindfulness and openness to God's transformative grace. It is his intentional response to God's invitation to a deeper relationship. It wears down his ego and deepens his cardiac spirituality. When he gets in his car for the Saturday trip, he is well aware it's an extension of his prayer—and without even thinking about it, a spiritual practice.

Spiritual practices shouldn't be a source of consternation or guilt. Whatever our practices and however they are done, they are both our acknowledgement of God's ardent longing and our response to God's invitation. They help promote mindfulness in the life of the ordinary mystic.

Practice

Reflect on your everyday life and think of something you do every day by rote or routine: brushing your teeth, talking to your spouse, taking the commuter train to work, washing the dishes, changing diapers, taking a walk, preparing a meal, or chatting with a friend. What awareness and intention would you need to make it a spiritual practice?

Do it tomorrow as a spiritual practice.

In the evening, assess its helpfulness to you.

Reflect

1. What are your current spiritual disciplines? Are they practiced daily, weekly, monthly, or yearly? How beneficial are they in making you mindful and responsive to God's transformative grace?

2. Which spiritual disciplines are challenging for you? Why? How can you rethink their practice?

Ponder

Any practice that promotes mindfulness of God's ardent longing and enthusiastic invitation to a deeper relationship is a spiritual discipline.

Chapter 13

STAYING AWAKE

MINDFUL LIVING

ow's your day going, Albert?" Manuel always asks the same question at the start of a phone call.

"Just the usual. I woke up, had breakfast, showered . . ."

"And checked your email. Then prayed. After your prayer, you checked your mailbox."

"How did you know?" I asked.

"Albert, you're a creature of habit. I bet you there isn't a person on this planet who doesn't know your daily routine. I bet I could do a Google search and find it mentioned somewhere on the web."

I chuckled—he was absolutely correct. I *am* a creature of habit. But I suspect I'm not the only one.

Many of us, unaware that God's ardent longing for a deeper relationship tries to touch and influence us, live like sleepwalkers. We wake up, drink coffee, eat breakfast, shower, go to work, eat our lunch, return home, have dinner, relax, go to bed—only to do it all over again tomorrow. We speak by rote and live by routine and repetition.

> John of the Cross says that God is the first contemplative. God's gaze on us makes us irresistibly attractive to him. So it is not we who first loved God, but God who first loved us. We wake up in the middle of a love story. We did not begin it.
>
> *John Welch, O Carm*

We need to wake from our dream state, come back to the present moment, and live with intentional mindfulness. Jesus challenges us, "Keep awake therefore, for you do not know on what day your Lord is coming" (Matthew 24:42). Paul too encourages the Thessalonians to live with mindfulness: "So then let us not fall asleep as others do, but let us keep awake and be sober" (1 Thessalonians 5:6). God speaks in Revelation, "See, I am coming like a thief! Blessed is the one who stays awake and is clothed, not going about naked and exposed to shame" (Revelation 16:15). These three biblical verses are vivid reminders that mindfulness does not happen by osmosis. It must be fostered by spiritual practices.

There is a simple, intentional strategy we can adopt that leads to mindful living and an awakened life. Answer the daily question, *What is God up to in my life?* Pondering and reflecting on what people say to us, the deepest feelings around the circumstances in our lives, our gut reactions to surprises and coincidences, and our most creative thoughts, especially those that seemingly come out of nowhere, remind us that God speaks through our lives. The four dimensions of human life—physical, mental, spiritual, and social—form the sacred arena where God expresses his ardent longing and enthusiastically invites us to a deeper relationship. We need to keep our ears to the ground and listen to our lives. Then we do our best to draw out the meaning and act on the message.

SPIRITUAL DIRECTION

Spiritual direction is a focused extension to that simple daily question, "What is God up to in my life?" It offers another aid to mindfulness. Far from mere faith sharing, this spiritual practice is a holy conversation that leads to divine revelation. The call of Samuel in 1 Samuel 3:1-10 epitomizes what can occur.

The novice Samuel was ministering in the temple under the more experienced Eli. Three times God called out to Samuel, and each time Samuel mistook the voice for Eli's, running to him and saying, "Here I am. You called me." On the third occasion, the spiritually experienced Eli perceived the voice of God. He offered the young Samuel wise advice: "Go, lie down; and if he calls you, you shall say, 'Speak, LORD, for your servant is listening'" (1 Samuel 3:9).

In a typical spiritual direction session, you bring the answer to that question, "What is God up to in my life?" The answer might include a word, a hunch, or an experience. It might be from the physical, mental, or social dimension—don't forget, the spiritual is immersed in those other three dimensions of our human experience. From these facts, you are asked questions such as, *How do you feel about that?* or *How are you coping with that?* Having expressed your feelings about the facts, you then move to the spiritual dimension, the realm of faith: you talk about the facts and feelings from a spiritual perspective. "In my frustration, God is challenging me to let go of my control issues and trust in him more deeply." "God is reminding me in this friendship that I am loved." "My gut tells me the Spirit is nudging me to take a stand against this injustice and speak out." As trust and vulnerability grow over time with your spiritual director, you open up and explore the entire treasure chest of your life experience. As you discuss their details, like Samuel, you sometimes discover the voice of God. Oral rumination uncovers divine revelation.

Born and raised in a multilingual family, Lucas has always enjoyed different cultural settings. For the past two years, he has occasionally daydreamed about making a three-year commitment to his church's mission in Guatemala. I remember the day he came for his spiritual direction appointment and mentioned that his senior pastor was asking for mission volunteers. Lucas was excited.

After telling me about his pastor's request and reminding me of his occasional daydream, he said, "I wonder if God is trying to tell me something."

"That's the million-dollar question, isn't it?"

"It sure makes sense in some ways. I've been toying with this idea of going on a mission for two years now. Pastor Mike's search for three volunteers is like a door of opportunity opening. I just don't know if this is my time . . ." Lucas paused and looked off into the distance.

Having heard the facts, I decided to move the conversation along to the second level of emotions as I asked him how he felt about that possibility.

He pondered the question for a while. "Nervous . . . and excited! I'm nervous because I've never done anything like this before. But I'm also excited because this could be a dream come true." Lucas paused again.

Our session ended on that note.

The following month, Lucas returned and began our time together with what I can only describe as an incredulous nervous smile. Speaking from a faith perspective, he said, "You won't believe it. I talked to my wife and I talked with Pastor Mike. I am as sure as I can possibly be that God has opened the door of opportunity and is calling me to Guatemala. Patty and I are leaving in three months."

My sessions with Lucas reminded me yet again how God is constantly calling us to a deeper relationship by steering and impacting our lives. They also reminded me of the benefits I myself have experienced as a directee in spiritual direction.

I was in my early twenties when I first committed to the practice of spiritual direction. I was a bit nervous and didn't know what to expect. I was also suspicious and leery over the prospect of giving control of my life over to a director who really didn't know me.

> **"My director told me to do it" can never justify a course of action. The person who receives direction must always retain personal responsibility, and the mode and content of sound direction will help a person to retain and develop personal responsibility, not make it more difficult.**
>
> *William A. Barry and William J. Connolly*

"I would be too!" my director, Sr. Theresa, said. "Your life belongs to God, not to me. So many people wrongly presume that a spiritual director directs your life like a conductor directing different parts of an orchestra. But that's not my role as a spiritual director—nor would I presume to tell you how to live *your* life. I'm a spiritual director in another sense. My role is to *direct your attention* to the many ways the Spirit might be moving in your life. By asking you open-ended questions such as 'What is God saying to you in that feeling?,' 'Where do you experience the call to growth right now?,' 'When did you last experience God like that?,' 'What do you think God might be inviting you to do in this situation?,' 'How are you praying with this experience?,' I try to clarify and heighten your awareness of God's longing in the nitty-gritty of your daily schedule. And then we discuss how best you can respond to that grace."

Over the past forty years, I've found St. Theresa's understanding of what it means to be a spiritual director has held true with all my subsequent spiritual directors. Each one, in his or her own unique way, has helped me grow in the awareness of God's presence in my life. Each has affirmed and sometimes challenged me on my spiritual journey. Occasionally each has taught me a prayer technique or given me another perspective. Each has kept me accountable and helped me to listen to God's invitation in the four dimensions of my life. And in dark and difficult times, each has been a companion and a witness to God's presence.

EMBRACE AMBIGUITY

In a world that applauds an independent, take-charge attitude and celebrates power as a sword to be wielded, staying awake and living mindfully are countercultural: they promote humility and what I consider to be the highest form of mystical prayer, "Thy will be done." Staying awake and mindfulness call us to let go of rigid control of our lives and allow the Spirit of God to shape and guide us. That sometimes means pitching a tent in what feels like the middle of nowhere and at other times, putting one foot in front of the other even when we don't know the final destination. It requires patience and waiting.

> The principle guide [on the spiritual journey] is the Holy Spirit.
> John of the Cross

After spending twelve years living out of a suitcase as an itinerant preacher and accumulating 1.3 million frequent flyer miles on United Airlines, I became weary of being in a different city and preaching in a different church every week. I found myself occasionally day-dreaming about settling down and having some stability in my life. However, I still felt called to the preaching ministry and the ministry of training future spiritual directors.

Out of the blue, I received a phone call from the director of Cedarbrake Catholic Retreat Center in Temple, Texas. Over the years, I had preached many retreats there and offered continuing education for spiritual directors in the Catholic diocese of Austin where the retreat center is located. "Bishop Joe and I were wondering if you would like to become the new chaplain for our retreat center. You would be a member of our retreat team as well as help with our training of future spiritual directors."

I was dumbfounded. *Was this God's way of teasing me, answering a prayer I hadn't even prayed, or a temptation from the devil?* "Let me get back to you," was my breathless response. I hung up.

I told my spiritual director about this intriguing offer. After mentioning that I didn't know if this was truly the will of God, I said, "God is going to have to make it absolutely clear if I am being called to the retreat house."

"That's not going to happen, Albert," Fr. Ralph replied as he chuckled under his breath. "It's only under the rarest of circumstances with the most hardheaded of persons that God knocks someone off a high horse and gives clear marching orders. The vast majority of times, God simply tries to persuade and entice rather than prescribe and decree. Responding to God is a slippery slope, because each possible decision has its own advantages and disadvantages. Sooner or later, with the best of intentions, we make a decision in freedom and take a step in faith. And we don't count the cost. Sitting on the fence only leads to paralysis and anxiety."

> If you are fear-based and "worried about many things," as [Jesus]
> says in Luke 10:41, you don't have faith in a Biblical sense. Faith is
> to be able to trust that God is good, involved, and on your side.
>
> Richard Rohr, OFM

Fears typically justify our fence sitting. We dread the possibility of any physical pain or discomfort that might be associated with responding to God's invitation: *Will my life be as comfortable as it is now?* We cringe at the potential criticism that might be leveled against us: *Will my spouse, family, and friends blame me if I make a mistake?* We are apprehensive about possible disgrace: *Will I look like a fool? How will this affect my reputation?* All of these fears are expressions of the ego's obsessions.

"And, of course, there is the worry about whether or not this is the right thing to do," Fr. Ralph continued. "The important thing is not that we get it right. The fact is—we don't always. What's important is that we respond and keep walking in the direction we think or feel the Spirit is leading."

Fr. Ralph's advice reminded me that the spiritual journey is ongoing, and we never reach the final destination in this life. God is a "jealous God" (Exodus 20:5) and is always inviting us to a deeper relationship with all its costs. Accepting that invitation never cripples or diminishes us but leads us to freedom and fulfillment. We are continually challenged to step over the ego and take a faith-filled risk—and sometimes we make what we later discover to be a mistake. But God honors each and every decision, even a questionable or mistaken one, as long as it is made in faith. Staying awake and living mindfully isn't about being right; it's about taking a risk for God right here, right now, whatever the cost.

FREEDOM FROM THE EGO

Living mindfully *is* costly, because it requires disengaging and ignoring the ego with its fixation on self-concern, self-image, self-gratification, and self-preservation. The ego and its obsessions are the source of so much stress and anxiety.

Luke 10 contains a famous incident in the life of Jesus. Jesus is welcomed into the home of Martha, who lives with her sister Mary. While Martha is responding to the necessary tasks of hospitality, Mary sits listening at the feet of Jesus. Martha complains to Jesus about Mary's lack of cooperation and help. Jesus responds, "Martha, Martha, you are worried and distracted by many things; there is need of only one thing. Mary has chosen the better part, which will not be taken away from her" (Luke 10:41-42).

This story has traditionally been interpreted as highlighting the tension between the contemplative and active life, with the life of prayer being considered superior over action. But there is a deeper interpretation. While Martha's worry and distraction are rooted in her ego's preoccupations and demands, Mary has managed to silence hers and sits wide awake with a spirit of attentive mindfulness.

This deliberate disregard of the ego that Mary manifests does not come easily or quickly; it calls for a rewiring of our thinking as Jesus taught in the Sermon on the Mount. We slowly shed the ego-invested self, adopt the thinking of the Sermon on the Mount, and are born again: "You were taught to put away your former way of life, your old self, corrupt and deluded by its lusts, and to be renewed in the spirit of your minds, and to clothe yourselves with the new self, created according to the likeness of God in true righteousness and holiness" (Ephesians 4:22-24). This new self, unencumbered by the demands of the ego, allows us to live with mindfulness. It is the mystical me.

Soon after talking to Fr. Ralph, I began a thirty-day retreat, arranged a year earlier, in a hermitage in South Carolina. I am embarrassed to admit that I initially resisted the offer to become the chaplain of Cedarbrake Catholic Retreat Center. I arrogantly thought my "congregation" should be national and larger than the diocese of Austin and the seventy-five acres that surround the retreat center. But as the days of solitude continued and I began to delve deeper, I slowly came to the realization that this was an answer to the prayer I had never explicitly prayed, "Lord, give me a home where I can preach and still feel the grass grow under my feet." Though I feared my Franciscan community would think I was foolish for throwing away such an exciting life of travel, I made the decision to accept the position. I haven't looked back and offer the risk I took as my gift to God.

Staying awake and living mindfully are two fundamental challenges and tasks of becoming an ordinary mystic. They require continual attention and reflection as we go within and ponder God's ardent longing and enthusiastic invitation voiced in the nitty-gritty details of our daily lives. Then, to avoid narcissistic self-absorption, we stretch ourselves and respond with the cardiac spirituality of Jesus: surrender, sacrifice, and service. This dynamic interplay between divine grace and human action becomes as natural as inhaling and exhaling in the life of an ordinary mystic.

Practice

Visit www.sdiworld.org, the website for Spiritual Directors International. Click on the "Seek and Find Guide." Spend time reading the articles on the left-hand side of the screen. Pay particular attention to the articles entitled, "Spiritual Direction 101" and "Questions to Ask a Potential SD."

Fill out the "Seek and Find" form in the center of the screen. Click submit and notice the names of spiritual directors in your area.

Spend time pondering whether or not God is calling you to commit to spiritual direction as a way of staying awake and living mindfully. If the answer is yes, contact two or three potential spiritual directors and interview each.

If one spiritual director stands out and you feel a connection to him or her, commit to spiritual direction.

Reflect

1. Think back to a time when you experienced God's ardent longing in the physical, mental, spiritual, or social dimension of your life and were convinced God was calling you to a deeper relationship. How did you know it was God? How did you respond?

2. When has the need to be certain made you hesitate to respond to God's enthusiastic invitation? What worries, fears, or ego obsessions circulated around that need?

Ponder

Staying awake and living mindfully do not happen by osmosis.

CONCLUSION

A personal, mysterious, and incomprehensible God of unconditional love ardently longs for us and enthusiastically invites
us to a deeper relationship. This is grace, and every dimension of
our human experience—physical, mental, spiritual, and social—sings
of it. Grace begins our transformation.

Our response to grace starts with waking up and living mindfully,
that childlike quality of living in the present moment. It is right here,
right now, that God calls us to intentionally respond to the unmet
need or required duty in front of us. Surrender, sacrifice, and service
are the essence of Jesus' cardiac spirituality and shape our heartfelt
response. It is also right here, right now, that God calls us to come
as we are to prayer. We respond with an honesty and transparency
that include our most uncomfortable emotions.

As we open our lives with all the baggage from our upbringing and
childhood, we grimace at our attachment to the ego and its four obsessions with self-concern, self-image, self-gratification, and self-preservation.
This fixation keeps us stuck in the past or tripping into the future. Jesus
the electrician brings us back to the present moment by rewiring our
thinking about true happiness and the ego obsessions in the Sermon
on the Mount. Together with a Jesus-inspired image of God and the
deliberate choice for forgiveness, the ego begins to deflate.

As the ego shrinks, our awareness of God's continual gift of grace
increases. That sensitivity is sharpened through prayer and the
practice of spiritual disciplines. We open ourselves at ever-deepening
levels to God time and again while our desires are transformed. We
begin to live the most mystical of prayers, "Thy will be done." And
with that, we discover our truest identity as ordinary mystics.

NOTES

1 RIGHT HERE, RIGHT NOW

7   *So often people say*: Leo Knowles, ed., *Catholic Book of Quotations* (Huntington, IN: Our Sunday Visitor Publishing Division, 2004), 49-50.

9   *Jesuit Jean-Pierre de Caussade*: It "seems almost impossible" that de Caussade was the author of the work. See Dominique Salin, SJ, "The Treatise on Abandonment to Divine Providence," *The Way*, 46/2 (April 2007), 21-36.

    De Caussade calls the present moment a "sacrament": Jean-Pierre de Caussade, *Abandonment to Divine Province*, trans. John Beevers (New York: Doubleday, Image, 1975), 24.

10 *Every moment we live*: De Caussade, *Abandonment to Divine Province*, 50.

10 *Do what you are doing*: Chris Lowney, "When Pope Francis Was Put On Laundry Duty," November 17th, 2013, http://religion.blogs.cnn.com/2013/11/17/when-pope-francis-was-put-on-laundry-duty.

11 *Each minute of life*: Fulton J. Sheen, *From the Angel's Blackboard: The Best of Fulton J. Sheen, A Centennial Celebration* (Liguori, MO: Triumph Books, 1995), 6.

12 *Super Soul Sunday*: The show aired October 29, 2017, on the Oprah Winfrey Network.

15 *Being present with full attention*: Mary Margaret Funk, OSB, *Discernment Matters: Listening with the Ear of the Heart* (Collegeville, MN: Liturgical Press, 2013), 82.

2 WHAT'S MISSING?

21 *The one with a large foundation*: Benedict J. Groeschel, CFR, *Spiritual Passages: The Psychology of Spiritual Development* (New York: Crossroad, 1983), 45.

23 *Our spiritual journey*: Thomas Keating, *Foundations for Centering Prayer and the Christian Contemplative Life [Open Mind, Open Heart; Invitation to Love; The Mystery of Christ]* (New York: Continuum, 2002), 135.

26 *We need [discernment]*: Pope Francis, *Gaudete et Exsultate: On the Call to Holiness in Today's World*, 50, http://w2.vatican.va/content/francesco/en/apost_exhortations/documents/papa-francesco_esortazione-ap_20180319_gaudete-et-exsultate.html, #169.

3 JESUS THE ELECTRICIAN

36 *The emphasis in Jesus' ministry*: Thomas Keating, *Foundations for Centering Prayer and the Christian Contemplative Life [Open Mind, Open Heart; Invitation to Love; The Mystery of Christ]* (New York: Continuum, 2002), 333.

40 *Eventually we reach a point*: Ronald Rolheiser, "Moving Beyond 'Our Little Rule,'" July 9, 2002, http://ronrolheiser.com/moving-beyond-our-little-rule.

4 CARDIAC SPIRITUALITY

49 *Once for all*: Augustine of Hippo, *Homilies on the First Epistle of John*, vol. III/14, *The Works of Saint Augustine: A Translation for the 21st Century*, translated by Boniface Ramsey (New York: New City Press, 2008), 110.

50 *Love in fact is the spiritual life*: Thomas Merton, *The Wisdom of the Desert: Sayings from the Desert Fathers of the Fourth Century* (New York: New Directions, 1961), 17.

The most certain sign: St. Teresa of Avila, *The Interior Castle*, 5.3.8, in *The Collected Works of St. Teresa of Avila*, translated by Kieran Kavanaugh, OCD, and Otilio Rodriguez, OCD, vol. 2, *The Way of Perfection; Meditations on the Song of Songs; The Interior Castle* (Washington, DC: ICS, 1980), 351.

53 *When evening comes*: St. John of the Cross, *Sayings of Light and Love*, 60, in *The Collected Works of St. John of the Cross*, translated by Kieran Kavanaugh, OCD, and Otilio Rodriguez, OCD (Washington, DC: ICS, 1991), 90.

5 INSIDES OUT

61 *We think God is like a parent*: Ronald Rolheiser, OMI, "Struggling in Prayer," in Robert J. Wicks, general editor, *Prayer in the Catholic Tradition: A Handbook of Practical Approaches* (Cincinnati, OH: Franciscan Media, 2016), 92–93.

62 *The Welcoming Prayer*: Cynthia Bourgeault, *Centering Prayer and Inner Awakening* (Cambridge, MA: Cowley, 2004), 141-52.

63 *nudgings of God*: Gerard Hughes, *God of Surprises* (London: Darton, Longman & Todd, 1988), x.

64 *common challenging emotions*: These insights come from Evelyn Eaton Whitehead and James D. Whitehead, *Transforming Our Painful Emotions: Spiritual Resources in Anger, Shame, Grief, Fear, and Loneliness* (Maryknoll, NY: Orbis, 2010).

6 A FINICKY GOD

69 *Spiritual consolation is experienced*: Margaret Silf, *Inner Compass: An Invitation to Ignatian Spirituality* (Chicago, IL: Loyola Press, 2007), 88.

71   *A person dwells in a state of desolation*: Vinita Hampton Wright, "Consolation and Desolation," IgnatianSpirituality.com, www.ignatianspirituality.com /25557/consolation-and-desolation-2, accessed July 8, 2018.

74   *I am told God lives in me*: Mother Teresa of Calcutta, quoted in Emily Stimpson Chapman, "Understanding the 'Dark Night of the Soul,'" OSV Newsweekly, May 20, 2015, www.osv.com/OSVNewsweekly/Story /TabId/2672/ArtMID/13567/ArticleID/17512/Understanding-the-'dark -night-of-the-soul'-.aspx.

     Mother Teresa's private letters: Brian Kolodiejchuk, MC, ed., Mother Teresa, *Come Be My Light: The Private Writings of the "Saint of Calcutta"* (New York: Doubleday, 2007).

7 GROPING IN THE DARK

80   *Nothing new happens*: Richard Rohr, "Days Without Answers in a Narrow Space," *The National Catholic Reporter*, February 1, 2000, 15.

81   *Some people will never learn anything*: Anthony de Mello, *The Heart of the Enlightened* (New York: Doubleday, 1989), 159.

82   *[humans] must keep their eyes shut*: St. John of the Cross, *The Dark Night*, 2.16.12, in *The Collected Works of St. John of the Cross*, translated by Kieran Kavanaugh, OCD, and Otilio Rodriguez, OCD (Washington, DC: ICS, 1991), 434.

83   *People who have really met the Holy*: Richard Rohr, "Utterly Humbled by Mystery," On Being blog, November 6, 2017, https://onbeing.org/blog /richard-rohr-utterly-humbled-by-mystery.

     Father, I abandon myself: Cathy Wright, LSJ, *Charles de Foucauld: Journey of the Spirit* (Boston, MA: Pauline Books & Media, 2005), 78.

87   *My Lord God*: Thomas Merton, *Thoughts in Solitude* (New York: Farrar, Straus, and Cudahy, 1958), 83.

8 CHALLENGING THE EGO

92   *Forgiving does not mean forgetting*: Henri J. Nouwen, "Healing Our Memories," Henri Nouwen Society, http://henrinouwen.org/meditation /healing-our-memories.

96   *We need a theology*: Ronald Rolheiser, OMI, as quoted in Leo Knowles, ed., *Catholic Book of Quotations* (Huntington, IN: Our Sunday Visitor Publishing Division, 2004), 140.

98   *The parable is not just about the Prodigal Son*: Thomas Keating, *Foundations for Centering Prayer and the Christian Contemplative Life [Open Mind, Open Heart; Invitation to Love; The Mystery of Christ]* (New York: Continuum, 2002), 294.

9 INSPIRED BY JESUS

104   *her compass was determined by personal, religious, and cultural factors*: Some of
these factors are briefly mentioned in Sue Pickering, *Spiritual Direction:
A Practical Introduction* (Norwich: Canterbury Press, 2008), 43.

One day, Angelica spread out all her crayons: Mary M. McGlone, "The Image of
God," National Catholic Reporter, September 30, 2017, www.ncronline.org
/news/spirituality/image-god.

106   *Our idea of God*: Thomas Merton, *New Seeds of Contemplation*, Shambhala
Library (Boston: Shambhala, 2013), 17.

108   *God, by definition*: Ronald Rolheiser, "The Richness of the Mystery of God,"
RonRolheiser.com, May 30, 2010, http://ronrolheiser.com/the-richness-of
-the-mystery-of-god.

God is a great underground river: Meister Eckhart, as quoted in Leo Knowles,
ed., *Catholic Book of Quotations* (Huntington, IN: Our Sunday Visitor Publishing Division, 2004), 152.

If you understand it: Augustine of Hippo, *Serm.* 52:6; *Serm.* 117:3.

109   *the inexpressible: Liturgy of St. John Chrysostom*, Anaphora.

10 LIFE, WORDS, SILENCE, AND ACTION

118   *For mental prayer*: St. Teresa of Avila, *The Book of Her Life*, 8.5, in *The Collected
Works of St. Teresa of Avila*, translated by Kieran Kavanaugh, OCD, and
Otilio Rodriguez, OCD, vol. 1, *The Book of Her Life; Spiritual Testimonies*
(Washington, DC: ICS, 1976), 96.

122   *Praying is no easy matter*: Henri Nouwen, "First, Unclench Your Fists," BeliefNet,
www.beliefnet.com/faiths/2006/06/first-unclench-your-fists.aspx?,
accessed July 11, 2018.

123   *The one who sings*: Augustine of Hippo, *Enarrat. Ps.* 72, 1.

Prayers in stone: See the photographic coffee-table book by Alexander
Liberman, *Prayers in Stone* (New York: Random House, 1997).

127   *Do not be too anxious*: Thomas Merton, *The Inner Experience: Notes on Contemplation*, edited with introduction by William H. Shannon (New York:
HarperOne, 2003), 98.

11 EARS TO THE GROUND

132   *Do not make the mistake*: Thomas Merton, *The Inner Experience: Notes on Contemplation*, edited with introduction by William H. Shannon (New York:
HarperOne, 2003), 98.

12 PRACTICAL PRACTICES

140 *For often when a person is distracted*: St. Teresa of Avila, *The Interior Castle*, 6.2.2, in *The Collected Works of St. Teresa of Avila*, translated by Kieran Kavanaugh, OCD, and Otilio Rodriguez, OCD, vol. 2, *The Way of Perfection; Meditations on the Song of Songs; The Interior Castle* (Washington, DC: ICS, 1980), 367.

142 *The various disciplines of the spiritual life*: Henri J. M. Nouwen, *Spiritual Formation: Following the Movements of the Spirit* (New York: HarperOne, 2015), 18.

143 *A saint is a person who*: Thomas Merton, "The Vow of Conversion" (Kansas City, MO: Credence Cassettes), tape AA 2228.

144 *the "soul of prayer"*: "Fasting Quotes," Daily Devotions for Dining with God, February 15, 2015, www.diningwithgod.org/fasting-quotes-catholic-popes -and-saints-3.

   Fasting cleanses the soul: This translation comes from *The Summa Theologiae of St. Thomas Aquinas*, 2nd and rev. ed., translated by Fathers of the English Dominican Province, 1920. Online edition available at www.newadvent .org/summa/3147.htm. The Augustine citation is *De orat. et Jejun* (Serm. lxxii [ccxxx, *de Tempore*]).

   We must be careful: Pope Francis, Homily, March 5, 2014, as quoted at Kevin Cotter, "What Should I Do for Lent? Pope Francis' 10 Tips," Focus, February 22, 2017, https://focusoncampus.org/content/what-should-i -do-for-lent-pope-francis-10-tips.

147 *Let all guests who arrive be received as Christ*: *The Rule of St. Benedict*, translated by Rev. Boniface Verheyen (United Kingdom: Aziloth Books, 2012), 68.

13 STAYING AWAKE

152 *John of the Cross says*: John Welch, O Carm., "Prayer in the Carmelite Tradition," *Prayer in the Catholic Tradition*, 219.

155 *"My director told me to do it"*: William A. Barry and William J. Connolly, *The Practice of Spiritual Direction, Revised and Updated* (New York: HarperOne, 2009), 11.

156 *The principle guide [on the spiritual journey]*: St. John of the Cross, *The Living Flame of Love*, 3.46, in *The Collected Works of St. John of the Cross*, translated by Kieran Kavanaugh, OCD, and Otilio Rodriguez, OCD (Washington, DC: ICS, 1991), 691.

158 *If you are fear-based*: Richard Rohr, *Jesus' Plan for a New World: The Sermon on the Mount* (Cincinnati, OH: St. Anthony Messenger Press, 1996), 118.

formatio
TRADITION. EXPERIENCE.
TRANSFORMATION.

Formatio books from InterVarsity Press follow the rich tradition of the church in the journey of spiritual formation. These books are not merely about being informed, but about being transformed by Christ and conformed to his image. Formatio stands in InterVarsity Press's publishing tradition by integrating God's Word with spiritual practice and by prompting readers to move from inward change to outward witness. InterVarsity Press uses the chambered nautilus for Formatio, a symbol of spiritual formation because of its continual spiral journey outward as it moves from its center. We believe that each of us is made with a deep desire to be in God's presence. Formatio books help us to fulfill our deepest desires and to become our true selves in light of God's grace.